Building an Intermediate Program

By
LUCILE DESJARDINS

A Textbook in the Standard Leadership
Curriculum, Outlined and Approved by
the International Council of Religious
Education

Printed for the
LEADERSHIP TRAINING PUBLISHING ASSOCIATION

by

THE WESTMINSTER PRESS
Philadelphia

Printed in the United States of America

FOREWORD

INTERMEDIATES — twelve to fourteen years of age — are in fact "the in-between-ones." Between childhood on the one hand and adulthood on the other, these young people face many difficult adjustments. Sometimes their elders have left them a sorry and confusing heritage. Often, however, their elders have companioned with young people, brimful of possibilities as they are, and have linked their lives together in a mutual quest for God and brotherhood. This mutual questing offers much of promise for the future. When men and women are pals with their Intermediates, the results are significant for young and old alike.

Many Intermediates glimpse the meaning of the Church in redeemed lives and the Christian world community. Their parents, their counselors, and their teachers work hard to make real the great ministry of service needed and provided by churches and denominations. Fortunate indeed are they whose lives come thus to glow with a great appreciation and a great purpose. The future belongs to them.

One of the chief concerns of Protestantism is with the development of persons who are dependable, who have inner control, an inner voice, an authority to believe, to interpret, to dare, to live greatly. It will not be enough in the future to offer programs that seek primarily to transmit. The teacher may well be the leader, the counselor, but never the boss. There is no place for the dictator spirit in teaching young children. It will not do with Intermediates. These inner con-

trols come as the mature counselor provides opportunity for choice and action.

"Building an Intermediate Program" gives a
wealth of practical resources for all who deal with this
very important age. Miss Lucile Desjardins has had
a rich background of training and experience and firsthand contact with Intermediate boys and girls. She
has brought together in a very readable way helps and
insights for building the program for this commonly
"hard-to-hold" group that will enable many parents,
leaders, and counselors to enlist the interest and activity of one of the finest age groups in the world in the
challenging adventure of developing Christian lives
and a Christian brotherhood in a redeemed world.

NATHANIEL F. FORSYTH,
*Chairman, Editorial-Educational
Committee of the Leadership
Training Publishing Association.*

CONTENTS

INTRODUCTION

IN A certain city of the Midwest may be seen the sculptured form of a pioneer boy and his mother.[1] Clothed in quaint pioneer garb, they remind us of the days which have almost vanished from our American life. They look as though they were ready to step forward, hand in hand, toward some distant goal which the mother has in her mind. The child walks willingly beside his adult guide.

On an eastern college campus stands another bronze model, a tablet [2] fashioned in memory of the loved educator, Alice Freeman Palmer. In this tablet the figure of the woman represents the college or alma mater. She is in the act of sending a young woman graduate forth into the world. The young woman's eyes are fixed eagerly on a distant goal. She pauses for one moment of farewell before she steps forth from the shelter of college walls and from the shelter which a great teacher's personal guidance affords — out to meet the storms, the baffling difficulties, the perplexing problems, the terrific temptations, which she must face independently as a mature person with the resources which fifteen or more years of education should have given her.

One other figure is needed to make this trilogy complete. This is to be found in the children's playground in Providence, Rhode Island, where the sculptor, Gail

[1] The Pioneer Woman, by Bryant Baker.
[2] The Alice Freeman Palmer Memorial Tablet, by Daniel Chester French. Go Preach, by Burnand, might be substituted for this.

Sherman Corbett, has fashioned the figure of a half-grown adolescent girl, reaching backward with one hand to clasp the familiar block of the past which represents security and at the same time reaching forward shyly but adventurously toward the future to taste the satisfactions, the achievements, and the recognitions which adult life may bring.

Let this half-grown figure, reaching back furtively for childhood securities and at the same time reaching uncertainly but eagerly toward the new experiences of youth, stand as a symbol for all those early adolescent [3] boys and girls who are to be found in the seventh, eighth, and ninth grades or in the junior high schools and in the Intermediate or Pioneer Departments of our churches. Let this figure stand for these perplexing, intriguing, interesting younger adolescents, who, though only half mature, wish very much to be treated like grown-up folks. They are indeed a challenge to the Christian Church. They are the pioneers of the new days which we have faith to believe lie ahead and for the new world which is to come.

But the world which these pioneers face is very different from the world which the pioneer mother faced

[3] Several terms are used to indicate boys and girls from twelve to fourteen years of age, all of which are unsatisfactory. These terms are: "early adolescents," "junior high school group," "Intermediates," and "Pioneers." They will be used interchangeably in this book. Several denominations use the term "Pioneer" for organizations designed to serve seventh, eighth, and ninth grade pupils. In some school systems the seventh and eighth and ninth grades are a separate administrative unit called the junior high school. In other systems the seventh and the eighth grades are the last two years of grammar school and the ninth grade is the first year of the high school.

with her child or even the world which the young college woman faced several decades ago. The pioneer mother and son faced a wilderness to be conquered, a forest to be cleared, a home to be built and protected from wild animals, a living to be wrested from the soil. They were forced to fight a battle against the elements, often living far apart from their neighbors. In that sense they might be called " rugged individualists." But they discovered early the need of co-operative effort, for in their journey westward they traveled in wagon trains and often found it necessary to band together for protection against the Indians.

The growing lad of today, however, faces a different world. He must live in the society of his fellows, often in the congested sections of a great city. He will find it difficult to travel to any spot so isolated that he will not be within easy reach of his fellow beings. The way he learns, or fails to learn, to work and play with others will often determine his success or failure in life. The fields of his conquest will probably be social rather than geographical. He will need to learn how to live peacefully with those of other nationalities, races, and stations of life in co-operative social groups. More difficult still, he will need to learn how to live successfully in a society which has not yet been established on a co-operative basis. He must face war as a foe, with its ruthless exploitation of youth; racial prejudice; materialism; economic injustice; and unchristian ideals in business and politics. But he is also growing up in a world where such practices are being questioned as never before. As a Christian, he must decide for himself what attitude toward them he will take.

Members of the older generation will not be able to decide all these problems for youth. While, in some cases, they may point to a better way, they cannot travel the road for youth. Nor will the older generation be able to chart the paths in the new world which lies ahead. The youth must break new roads. He must hew out trails through the unexplored and untamed jungles of our half-pagan civilization into the new world which lies beyond. He must help to bring order out of chaos. He is a pioneer, soon to be entrusted with the responsibility of helping to build the Kingdom of peace, love, and good will among men.

By helping boys and girls to live richly, wisely, and religiously in the present; by helping them to solve the problems and to make the choices which are thrust upon them today; by exposing them to the stimulating lives of great-hearted, Christian men and women of the past and of the present; and, most of all, by introducing them to Jesus, the great Pioneer of all the ages, we may help them to become worthy citizens of the future.

CHAPTER I

GETTING ACQUAINTED WITH YOUNGER ADOLESCENTS

HAVE you started to read this book because you are interested in some live boys and girls of early adolescent age? Possibly you have responsibility for their guidance, either as a parent or as a Church School teacher or as a club or society leader. Do some of these boys and girls perplex you? Do you sometimes wish that you understood them better? Perhaps you are concerned about getting and holding their attention and interest during the class session. Or, as a parent, you have been able to hold your child's confidence up to this point, but now you feel him slipping away from you. Some of his actions and attitudes seem quite baffling to you. You would like to know how to become a real friend and guide to these boys and girls during these years when they are growing up so rapidly.

Let us take a look at these boys and girls we are seeking to reach and hold. Here is something for you to try. At the head of each column below place a letter or initial which will stand for a boy or a girl of Intermediate age whom you know. Then place a check in the column below this initial opposite each characteristic which you have especially noticed in this particular person. For example, if fourteen-year-old John in your club group seems to you to be growing rapidly, to be awkward, and to be lazy, place a "J" in the first

1

bracket and check marks down the column opposite
each of these characteristics.

THE YOUNGER ADOLESCENTS I KNOW BEST HAVE THE
FOLLOWING CHARACTERISTICS

	( )	( )	( )	( )
Rapid physical growth.	—	—	—	—
Self-consciousness.	—	—	—	—
Awkwardness.	—	—	—	—
Silliness, giggling.	—	—	—	—
Listlessness, laziness.	—	—	—	—
Bodily restlessness.	—	—	—	—
Self-assertiveness.	—	—	—	—
Thoughtlessness.	—	—	—	—
Sensitiveness to opinions of others.	—	—	—	—
Wide range of interest.	—	—	—	—
Sense of guilt.	—	—	—	—
Cliquishness.	—	—	—	—
	—	—	—	—
	—	—	—	—

Fill in the blank spaces above with other characteristics which you have noticed. Are the same boys and
girls interested in the same things which appealed to
them a few years ago? In what ways have their interests changed? Which of the following interests
have you noticed recently in the same younger adolescents?

INDIVIDUAL INTERMEDIATES I KNOW ARE MOST INTERESTED IN

Chums.	( )
Movies.	( )
Athletics.	( )
Future Vocation.	( )
Boy friends, girl friends (opposite sex).	( )
Reading (kind).	( )
Hobbies (name).	( )

Music (vocal or instrumental). ( )
Dancing. ( )
Handicraft projects. ( )
Public school activities, clubs, et cetera. ( )
Club activities outside school. ( )
Art. ( )
Religious questions. ( )
Standards for conduct. ( )
_____ ( )
_____ ( )

Add to this list other things which you know interest boys and girls of Intermediate age. Which of these dominant interests are taken into consideration in the planning of the Intermediate program for your church? Place a check (✓) before these in the list above. What other agencies of the community are taking these interests into account?

Bearing in mind the special characteristics and interests of the younger adolescents you know best, which of the following do you consider are the most imperative needs of these boys and girls? You might discuss this question with other Church School teachers or with parents. Then check the five needs which you consider most important. Add in the blank space following the list any other needs which you think should be included.

I Believe that Younger Adolescents Need

Wholesome group life. ( )
Stronger control or discipline in the home. ( )
Wholesome intimate friendships. ( )
More time to devote to church program. ( )
Christian standards for the evaluation of movies, reading material, radio programs, et cetera. ( )
More of a place in the life of the church. ( )
A decision to follow Christ. ( )

Greater knowledge of the Bible.   ( )
Inspiring personal heroes.   ( )
Help in solving personal problems.   ( )
Release from parental domination.   ( )
Greater respect for sacred things.   ( )
More satisfactory religious concepts.   ( )
More wholesome community recreational life.   ( )
Better co-operation between home and church and
     school.   ( )
Guidance in making choices.   ( )
Help in making social adjustments.   ( )
——————————————————————————————   ( )
——————————————————————————————   ( )

Which of the following do you think are the most
effective ways of getting to know boys and girls best?
In the following list check the methods which you
think might be used most helpfully in your own situation. Place two check marks opposite those which you
have actually used successfully.

EFFECTIVE WAYS OF GETTING TO KNOW YOUNGER ADOLESCENTS
ARE

Personal conversations on informal occasions.   ( )
Visits to homes; talks with parents.   ( )
Observing boys and girls on playground or at parties.   ( )
A visit to the public school they are attending.   ( )
Informal discussion in class on everyday problems and
     matters of interest to group.   ( )
The use of objective tests (for attitudes, information,
     concepts, interests, et cetera).   ( )
Sharing a hiking or camping experience with a group.   ( )
Reading books on adolescent psychology.   ( )
Recalling one's own days of adolescence.   ( )
——————————————————————————————   ( )

Add to this list other ways you have found helpful.
Then select one of these methods which seems to you
the most practicable and plan to use it within the next

few weeks in getting to know some boys and girls better.

A very helpful method is to keep a personal record of some of these boys and girls over a period of time. Include in it all the information, the insights which you gain from time to time which help you to understand the boy or girl as an individual. What are some of the things you might wish to find out about the home situation? About their use of leisure time, interests, hobbies, et cetera?

These Intermediates

All over this country each Sunday morning large and small groups of Intermediate boys and girls will be found attending Church Schools. These boys and girls come from many different homes. During the week they will be attending grammar schools or junior high schools. They will be found engrossed in well-planned club activities or using their leisure time in desultory activities of their own choosing. Teachers and parents and club leaders will find that, both in physical development and in social interests, the girls are for the present ahead of the boys. Teachers may often be baffled by the variation in interests and abilities displayed by one small group as well as by differences in stature and in other aspects of physical development. Church School teachers will probably be discouraged and puzzled because on one Sunday their groups seem very enthusiastic about proposed plans and on the next Sunday they have lost all interest in the projects they have undertaken. But at least the following six things will stand out as characteristic of most younger adolescents:

An interest in social life.

A desire to conform with their group.

A desire to belong to clubs and other organizations.

A desire to carry out worth-while enterprises.

A distaste for doing things the way children do them.

Awkwardness in social techniques.

Present Needs of Younger Adolescents

Many teachers will agree that the following, at least, are vital needs of growing boys and girls:

Guidance in the new experiences they are facing.

A religious interpretation of these experiences.

Teachers and leaders with real insight and understanding.

Exposure to inspiring personalities.

Wholesome group life.

Worthy causes to which they may give themselves in loyalty.

A vital place in the Christian Church.

Guidance in Everyday Experiences

Jim is thirteen years old. On Sunday morning when he dresses up in his long pants and ushers in Church School he appears quite grown-up. But before night comes he is very often quarreling in a most childish way with a smaller brother over some toy that he would be ashamed to have his school friends see him manipulating.

" Now that I am become a man, I have put away childish things." Thus wrote Paul to the church members in Corinth who, in the first century, had been acting somewhat childishly. Perhaps Paul looked back into his own youth and recalled a time when he was neither child nor man but a contradictory mixture of both. Perhaps the words which he wrote to the church at Philippi might also be applied to early adolescents, both in the first and in the twentieth centuries: " Forgetting the things which are behind, . . . I press on toward the goal."

In the very nature of the case, this pressing forward, leaving childhood behind, means an abundance of new experiences. Change and the adjustment to new situations are the very stuff out of which adolescent personality is woven. This new and changing social world into which adolescents are thrust is very challenging and appealing, but also bewildering in its complexity. In the midst of unfamiliar experiences younger adolescents need tactful guidance.

Only listen for a while to a buzzing group of girls trying to decide what is the " proper " thing to do at an informal reception to which they have been invited, or to a bunch of boys discussing how to go about building their first log cabin or their first amateur radio set. In these situations you will find every evidence of deep and genuine concentration upon the problem at hand. Have you ever wished that you might have the same kind of attention to the Sunday School lesson on Sunday morning?

Every real situation faced by an individual or a group, which has in it new and unfamiliar elements, requires this kind of reflective thinking, for new ways of responding or of acting must be sought out. In a situation like this it is helpful to know what other people have done in the past or in the present. Witness the eagerness with which the boys building a radio

set will turn to a description in Popular Mechanics
of how some other boy built a radio set, or notice how
eagerly girls will scan certain columns of newspapers
or magazines for information concerning correct social
usages.

Bob had the problem of summer vacation plans to
settle. His parents had given him the choice of staying at home and keeping his paper route through the
summer, thus earning enough money to buy for himself the bicycle he would need next fall to take him to
high school, or going with the family on a motor trip
through the East. His mother and father refused to
settle the question for him. However, with his dad's
help, he tried to look squarely at all angles of the situation. Finally he decided in favor of staying at home
and earning the bicycle. He knew that he had to have
it and he was sure that his dad could not afford to buy
it for him. He really felt quite grown-up and a real
member of the family when he finally made known to
them his decision.

Wise parents and leaders, like this father, will help
growing boys and girls to make their own decisions on
an increasing number of matters. They will help them
to study all the factors involved, stimulate them in a
search for possible results of their actions, and help
them in their search for any sources of information that
will throw light on the problem. Of course, if the decisions are to be truly Christian, somewhere in the
process the young adolescents will be challenged to
think of what Christ would have them do or of the
way truly Christian people have responded to the crises
they have faced. Under skillful Christian guidance,
any day may become for the adolescent a true " de-

cision day " for Christ and for the Christian way of living.

But the religious leader should be especially sensitive to those experiences to which boys and girls commit themselves with the greatest intensity. In these lies the greatest opportunity for the development of Christian personality. However, whether trifling or momentous, the choices being continually made by boys and girls determine the types of personality they are to achieve. A young person needs to achieve freedom as a responsible individual whose actions are guided, not by parental authority or domination or external compulsion of any kind, nor by the whims of " the crowd," but by worthy ideals and standards which have come to be accepted and cherished by the individual as his very own. It is only as this has been achieved that he is prepared to step out into the wider, more complex life of the community and the world as a mature personality able to guide his own life and influence the lives of others.

The Religious Interpretation of Everyday Experiences

In a certain community boys and girls were meeting every week in a nature club, conducted by a leader well versed in astronomy but with no great religious bent or interest. The teacher of the same boys and girls in the Church School sometimes wondered what she might do to lead them a step farther to an appreciation of the God who made the stars and is working through the laws of the universe. But she felt that a discussion on this subject might take the time which was needed for the regular Church School lesson. So she let her opportunity slip by while all the time the boys and girls were secretly wanting to discuss with her some religious questions which had arisen from their study of astronomy.

Perhaps you too, as a Christian teacher, have asked the question: " How can we hope to have anything to do with those experiences which take place outside the four walls of the church and Church School building? We have the group for only a half-hour period on Sunday morning, as a rule, and that seems a short enough time to teach the lesson for the day."

Does a Church School teacher have a responsibility of discovering these important everyday experiences and the questions which arise from them and of giving these special attention during the all too brief time of the Sunday morning session, helping boys and girls to interpret these and to discover a religious meaning in them? Or should the program for Intermediates in the Church School be concerned chiefly with a study and interpretation of Biblical experience, leaving untouched these everyday experiences of home, school, community, and playground? Or is this task of religious interpretation to be undertaken by the home through informal conversations which, it is to be hoped, parents are still having with their adolescent boys and girls? The answer to these questions will definitely influence the type of program to be developed for Intermediates in the church and the type of procedures to be used in class and club session.

A Need for Wise and Sympathetic Leaders

In the Federated Church in the Meadville Parish there are two teachers of Intermediate classes in the

Church School. The teacher of the girls' class is a
great worker in the community. She is on so many
committees that she does not have a great deal of time
to get acquainted with her girls. She wonders sometimes why they are so listless and inattentive on Sunday mornings and so irregular in attendance. On the
other hand, the boys' class has as its leader a young
man who enjoys the comradeship of younger boys. He
is always taking them on hikes and planning informal
times with them when they can really get acquainted
with each other. They feel that they can share with
him their ideas and their plans. The girls often wish
they had a teacher like that.

If guidance in everyday experiences is one of the
great needs of younger adolescents, may it not also be
said that a parallel need is for the kind of adult leader
who knows how, and has time, to " get next " to boys
and girls, to discover their interests and ideas, to
understand their problems, and to see in them their
real possibilities? Should not every Intermediate
teacher, then, voice the prayer, " Give thy servant . . .
an understanding heart "?

One fact which strikes the leader of boys and girls
of this age is their increased range of interests and
activities. Not so apparent on the surface is the great
variability in their abilities and in their emotional, social, and religious development. Observation shows
that variability is at a maximum at this age in almost
every ability of mind, sense, or muscle. One Christian
leader has written that any sentence beginning, " All
girls . . ." is a lie. Out of the failure of leaders to
recognize individual differences arises the feeling on
the part of some boys and girls that they are misunder-

stood. This difference public school educators are increasingly taking into consideration. They are beginning to realize as never before that real pupil needs
must be located by a slow and patient process of the
study of conduct and in the light of what educational
psychology has to say concerning the forces which play
upon the personality of the adolescent at this period
of life. Often apparent needs are merely symptoms
indicating some deeper-lying difficulty. Real guidance can be given only by an understanding, sympathetic adult who knows how to locate the roots of the
real difficulty and to appreciate personality possibilities.

Understanding the Problem Pupil

In almost every Church School department there are
likely to be several boys or girls who present behavior
difficulties and cause trouble within groups. These are
a source of discouragement and perplexity to the
leader. It is especially important that these " problem pupils " be thoroughly understood and the cause
of their reactions located. The outward behavior is
probably only a symptom of a deeper-rooted personality difficulty. With such pupils, case-study methods
should be used. All that can be discovered should be
found out about the complaint, the pupil himself, and
his environment, including home, school, and community factors. This calls for some personal counseling on
the part of the church leader.

Suggestions for Personal Counseling

The Department of Superintendence of the National
Education Association, through its Committee of

Character Education, offers the following practical suggestions for nonprofessional counselors [1]:

1. The best attitude is one of cheerful, thoughtful objectivity, avoiding pronounced sympathizing, condemnation, or an air of easy optimism. . . .

2. Remember the whole child. While you work for one character objective, take care lest you get undesirable by-products in other character objectives.

3. The child with extreme withdrawing, recessive characteristics is as much a problem in need of individual help as is the child with extreme aggressive characteristics. Too great shyness may mean more potential trouble than too great forwardness.

4. Utilize all readily accessible data, such as those relating to health, school progress, and home conditions. Cumulative pupil records already available in most schools furnish a large amount of valuable information.

5. Avoid treating symptoms. Try to find out why the child acts as he does and then fit the treatment to the cause of the difficulty.

6. In some cases the counselee should be kept informed of the purpose of the counselor, and should be appealed to consciously to aid in solving the problem. In other cases the counselee may be kept in partial or complete ignorance of the changes desired in him. . . .

7. Single experiences do not afford ground for generalization. Vivid incidents are particularly to be distrusted. Habitual and recurring behavior is the significant source of data.

8. Do not offer authoritative explanations. By the use of other cases and of questions, build up in the counselee his own reasonable interpretation of his behavior.

9. Expect patterns. Among the more common are dependence, fear of the new, avoidance of people, breakdowns, running away from a situation, projecting the blame onto an individual

---

[1] "Character Education," pages 251, 252. Tenth Yearbook of The Department of Superintendence. The Department of Superintendence of the National Education Association of the United States, 1932. Used by permission.

of a given type, and displacement, making a mountain out of a given molehill.

10. Do not give advice. Give the experience of yourself and others, so far as it is useful, taking particular care to emphasize the differences in the situation faced by the counselee. No two persons have faced exactly the same situation. What the counselee needs is ability to handle situations himself, not advice to follow.

11. Emphasize success rather than failure. Seek to arrange situations that will give the child a taste of success.

12. It is sometimes necessary to study other persons than the one immediately involved. A problem child means at least one and probably two problem parents.

13. It is seldom possible to depend exclusively upon the readjustment of the person and objects in the environment, or upon the new insight and attitude of the person being advised. Both are usually in need of some readjustment.

14. Keep confidences inviolate.

15. Avoid letting the plans focus on too distant goals without adequate attention to immediate steps. Help the counselee to plan on improving adjustment this week, not console himself with phantasy. The past and future exist to enrich the present.

16. Learn to identify early the cases which require a specialist, and be willing to refer them to him.

The Need for Exposure to Inspiring Personalities

Julia and Frances have the walls of their room covered with the latest pictures of their favorite movie stars. They are eager to see every film in which these favorite stars appear. They carefully study their way of dress and their mannerisms, and try to imitate them. Frank spends all his extra minutes up in the laboratory of his high school biology professor. He says he wants to be a biologist when he grows up. He admires greatly this young teacher, who takes time to answer his questions and to explain scientific things to him.

Many early adolescents are searching for patterns

according to which they may build their own lives. But abstract ideals can never meet the needs of these growing boys and girls. They must see these ideals embodied in concrete form, that is, in flesh and blood. They must see them fashioned in living personalities. So you will find these young people on a persistent quest for inspiring persons who will illustrate how effectively a person may live. Often their imitation of these, especially in the earlier years, will be merely conforming to externalities, but sooner or later the qualities of character their heroes possess will make an impression upon their lives.

Boys and girls find these life patterns in many places. For many, the motion pictures provide life patterns. Great athletes, explorers, and aviators capture many boyish imaginations. Characters in history and fiction may, for the book-loving youth, become even more powerful than living persons in influencing personality development. Fortunate indeed is the growing boy or girl who has been exposed to some of the most stimulating and inspiring personalities of the past centuries, who have dedicated their lives to great causes, who have lived adventurously for the right, not counting any cost too great a price to pay to maintain real integrity of character.

Inspiring Hebrew heroes whose stories we find in the pages of the Old Testament; early Christians who gave their lives joyously for their Christian faith; builders of the Christian Church through the centuries; creative lovers of beauty who have made their lasting contributions in religious art, music, and literature; missionaries who have bravely devoted their lives to the cause of the Kingdom in far-distant lands; daring pioneers in the field of social reconstruction who have caught a vision of better days ahead for the poor, the oppressed, the handicapped; others who have lived inspiringly in the face of tremendous handicaps — all these are the rightful heritage of every generation's youth. Fortunate are the boys and girls who find among these great personalities of history patterns for building their own lives. Real enrichment will come through vicariously sharing the experiences of " the great ones that are in the earth."

But supremely important is the exposure of boyhood and girlhood to that most dynamic, winsome, and inspiring of all personalities, Jesus Christ. Only as these others reflect the spirit and the personality of Jesus can their lives be called truly Christian. The supreme need, then, is exposure to this Personality in such a way that he will win the wholehearted allegiance of boys and girls so that they will commit their lives to him. Thus may Christ become the true pattern for their growing lives. Thus may his spirit and his way of responding to situations so capture their imaginations that his life may become " the way, and the truth, and the life " to them. The exposure of growing boys and girls to the commanding and inspiring personality of Christ lies at the very heart of the Christian educational program for this age. This should become the very heart of the educational program for the local church.

One word should also be said about the teacher himself and the pattern for living which he may give to the members of his class. Especially important at this age is the selection of teachers or leaders who will embody in their own lives the message and the teachings which they seek to make real on Sunday morning to their pupils. First and foremost, boys and girls are seeking to read " the gospel according to you." Through a dynamic, winsome Christian personality, more effectively than in any other way, may a leader guide youth to Christ, the supreme Personality.

Need for Wholesome Group Life

" I have to coax my boy to go to Sunday School," says one distressed mother. " He used to like to go, but now he says none of his crowd attends and why should he."

And the troubled teacher of Intermediates often asks the question, " What can I do to interest and hold the boys and girls in my class when they do not feel well acquainted with each other and meet only once a week on Sunday morning? "

It is very important that boys and girls of this age should have the chance of satisfying group fellowship with those of their own kind within the church setting. Unless this vital need is met by the church, these growing boys and girls are very apt to throw their interest and their loyalty where they can find this social need satisfied. Boy Scouts, Girl Scouts, and other clubs, by their very nature, succeed in forming or making use of natural or spontaneous groupings in a way the church has failed to do. Unless the leadership of the local church takes into account this strong social interest and desire to be with their own crowd, and provides wisely organized activities which will give natural groupings a chance, it is liable to struggle with the half-hearted loyalty and the irregular or forced attendance of junior high school boys and girls.

And this is not all. Group relationships need to be
broadened out. Unless boys and girls are to become
narrowly individualistic, religious and moral training
should also lay the sure foundations for effective participation in the great brotherhood of humanity, which
includes not only one's own family circle, one's group
of special friends in neighborhood and school, but also
persons belonging to every race in the world brotherhood.

Identification with a Great Cause

It is evident that the desire to belong to something
is one of the newly awakening interests of early adolescence. The desire to belong to something worth-while
is really a sign of growing up. Dean Russell Wicks,
in " The Reason for Living," says:

" You can tell when a person really outgrows this
childish stage when, out beyond anything which belongs to him, he finds some undertaking or cause of
which he can say, ' I belong to that.' The more significant the enterprise, the happier a man is in belonging to it with all his heart and soul." [2]

The Christian Church should offer to youth a great
cause to which boys and girls may yield their wholehearted loyalty. This cause is the Kingdom of God on
earth. Boys and girls need the opportunities the
Church affords for challenging Kingdom service. The
Christian Church should, therefore, provide for these
younger Christians a *real* place in the church program
of service in Kingdom-building.

The programs offered by the various youth organiza-

[2] Wicks, Russell, " The Reason for Living," page 7. Charles
Scribner's Sons, 1934. Used by permission.

tions outside the Church or within the Church will be
outgrown with the passing of the years. The Church
itself, however, claims a lifetime devotion. It presents
a cause which can never be outgrown. A " value center " is indispensable to every boy or girl if he is to
develop his highest potentialities. Through identification with the enlarging Kingdom program of the
Church, they may find their " value center " around
which their lives may be organized and integrated.
This process of integration will do more than anything
else to make their lives dynamic and effective.

The important problem, then, is how to build an
Intermediate program for growing adolescents which
will be thrilling and significant enough and so much
an integral part of the Church's total program for
Kingdom-building in community, country, and world
that boys and girls will be constrained to yield their
wholehearted loyalty to it.

But perhaps you may say: " I can get along all right
with individual Intermediates. It is when they get
together in a group that I am baffled." Our next chapter will deal with group life and relationships.

Suggestions for Further Reading and Study

Averill, Lawrence A., " Adolescence." Houghton Mifflin Com-
pany, 1936.
Boorman, W. Ryland, " Developing Personality in Boys."
The Macmillan Company, 1929.
Dimock, Hedley S., " Rediscovering the Adolescent." Associa-
tion Press, 1937.
Elliott, Grace L., " Understanding the Adolescent Girl." Henry
Holt and Company, Inc., 1930.
Gregg, Abel J., " Group Leaders and Boy Character." Associa-
tion Press, 1927.
Hollingworth, Leta S., " The Psychology of the Adolescent."
D. Appleton-Century Company, Inc., 1928.

Miller, Catherine Atkinson, "Leading Youth to Abundant Life," Chapters I and II. The Heidelberg Press, 1934.

Pechstein, L. A., and McGregor, A. L., "The Psychology of the Junior High School Pupil." Houghton Mifflin Company, 1924.

Sheridan, Alma S., "Teaching Intermediates in the Church School." The Methodist Book Concern, 1928.

Stewart, Frederick W., "A Study of Adolescent Development." The Judson Press, 1929.

Thom, D. A., "Guiding the Adolescent." Bureau Publication No. 225, Children's Bureau, United States Department of Labor. 10 cents.

"A Manual for Leaders of Intermediates," pages 10–16. Christian Board of Publication, St. Louis, Missouri, 1937.

CHAPTER II

CHRISTIAN GROUP LIFE FOR
INTERMEDIATES

HAVE you ever been troubled because of the dominating influence of some group outside the church upon the members of your class? Or, as parents, have you been perplexed because some club or clique or gang seems to demand the loyalty and time of your growing boys and girls? Have you studied the reasons for the popularity of these spontaneous groupings in your community? Is it due to the leadership they have within them, to their program of activities, to the close, friendly relationship existing among the members of the group, or to the dominating influence of one member of the group?

Or perhaps you have a class in the Church School made up of members coming from long distances who have no other opportunities during the week to meet with each other in a social way. You have been doing your best to weld this collection of individuals into a real social group, but you find it difficult because they have so few interests in common. Your problem is how to build a group spirit so that the members of the class will really feel at home with one another and enjoy thinking and working together. In what ways do you think this last can best be accomplished?

Perhaps you are conscious of practices and attitudes in the groups of boys and girls you know best which you feel fall below the ideal for Christian group life.

You would like to bring up the level of group life and relationships to a more nearly Christian level.

Consider each of the situations described below. What seems to you to be the difficulty in each case? Try to decide what would be the best way to improve each of these local church situations so that the group life involved would be more thoroughly wholesome and Christian. It may be helpful to discuss these cases with other teachers who are interested in junior high school boys and girls.

1. In a certain group in one local church the leader is quite carried away by modern ideas. She feels that boys and girls ought to manage their own department and classes. It happens that one girl who is rather aggressive is really running the department and getting quite a " kick " out of it. She has enough of a following to manage to get elected to important offices and she sees to it that her pals and cronies have the best chances to do things. If the department and classes seem a bit noisy and disorganized at times the leader consoles herself with the thought that they are at least busy and happy.

2. Another department has such a strong, attractive program that the boys and girls are vitally interested. Their departmental superintendent is a vigorous leader. The members of the group become so interested that they want to stay after the Sunday School hour and not attend the church services even though the pastor is planning part of the service especially for them.

3. In one group when the leader tries to get the members to talk and to express their own opinions freely on religious matters he gets no response. They

are perfectly willing to give back the answers expected of them, which involve factual information, but are not ready to think through a problem freely with him. If only he could recall, he would remember the time when the boys ventured to ask questions and made statements which seemed shocking to him. He told the boys that they ought not to have such thoughts — that they were sacrilegious.

4. In still another department in all the classes they are making notebooks on the lesson unit studied. Each girl is copying faithfully what her teacher tells her. The cover designs and the inside pages of all the notebooks are alike except for such differences as come from individual styles of writing or printing.

5. In another department the boys and girls are very quiet and orderly in worship and in their class session. They sit in order while their teachers " give them the lesson." Occasionally a teacher is surprised to find a pupil who has studied the lesson sufficiently to offer an intelligent answer to a question. When this happens, the teacher comments on the good co-operation in the home. No one in the group, however, seems to have any inclination or time to undertake any additional responsibility when something needs to be done for the department or the church. All say that they have too much to do at school and in their club.

6. In another class the teacher was away for one Sunday. The superintendent could find no one to undertake substituting for the absent teacher, so he suggested that the boys teach themselves. Coming in later, he discovered pandemonium in this particular corner of the room. The boys were engaged in a free-for-all scuffle.

Evaluate the group life of the boys and girls you know best — in their public school, in their Boy Scout or Girl Scout troop, in their Church School class or department, in their evening society group, in any other organized groups of which they are members. Measure it according to the standards which Christ would set for group life and relationships. (See pages 28–30 for a discussion of this.) Which of these groups exercises the dominant influence over their lives? Is this a constructive, character-building influence?

What changes do you think need to be made in your own class or society or club group if it is to be brought up to the Christian standard for group life?

Importance of Group Relationships

Group life is an amazingly important factor in the development of wholesome personality. A Saint Simeon Stylites on his lofty, lonely pillar in the desert or even a Robinson Crusoe with only his man Friday to keep him company has missed not only one of the satisfactions of abundant living but also one of the essential factors for character development.

This is particularly true in childhood and youth, when the foundations are being laid for wholesome personality. In a study by Hartshorne and May on the factors responsible for various character traits it was discovered that a child's associates influence him substantially in the development of moral ideas. They say that when the factors associated with consistency of conduct were investigated, it was discovered that consistency, when present, was a *function of group life and experience*.[1]

[1] Compare Hartshorne, Hugh; May, Mark; and Shuttle-

While the influence of parents on conduct was found to be the most powerful factor, the influence of associates was found to be more important than the influence of the public-school teacher, the Church School teacher, or the club leader. And this influence of associates became more marked as children grew older.

Importance of Group Life for Adolescents

The strategic importance of group life is made still more evident as it affects the lives of adolescent boys and girls. Students of personality believe that the adolescent is especially sensitive to the status that he holds among his associates. The urge for friendship, recognition, status, or approval is undoubtedly strong during these years. If wholesome personality is to be developed, there must be " at least a minimum satisfaction of the desire to be wanted, accepted, liked, approved, and appreciated by one's associates." [2]

The strong appeal of group life is shown in the " ganging together " of boys and girls. Whatever the meeting place may be, they find strength in numbers, either for useful enterprises or for destructive pranks. Conformity to the crowd seems, to many troubled parents, to be the one law to which their boys and girls yield implicit obedience. In many such gangs or cliques, the first steps are sometimes taken toward juvenile delinquency. On the other hand, group enterprises, group activity, group loyalty are important factors in social experience of the best sort.

worth, Frank, " Studies in the Organization of Character," page 98. Study III of " Studies in the Nature of Character." The Macmillan Company, 1930. Used by permission.

[2] Dimock, Hedley S., " Rediscovering the Adolescent," page 114. Association Press, 1937. Used by permission.

In the recent study by Hedley S. Dimock, the investigators found that:

> " The individual is strongly influenced by regular, frequent, and continuous experience in a group that has unity, morale, extensive interweaving of friendships, and other psychological qualities of cohesiveness. This kind of group experience does affect the personality status, the moral ideas, the specific behavior, the unity of ideals and conduct, and the integration or consistency of conduct of its members." [3]

And he goes on to state certain implications arising from this fact:

> " If these social forces are capitalized, they may become the allies of education and be directed toward the achievement of desirable outcomes in the development of persons. To ignore them in the educational task, if the personality and character results are counted important, is to work against tremendous odds." [3]

This same study divides the groups in which adolescents are to be found into two kinds, the primary and the secondary groups — the first characterized by " intimate, face-to-face association and co-operation " and a " fusion of individualities in a common whole " which results in " the sort of sympathy and mutual identification for which *we* is the natural expression "; and the other characterized by " indirect association and lacking psychological factors of oneness."

For practical purposes he divides the groups to which adolescents belong into: special interest groups (such as hobby clubs), clubs, purpose groups, natural or neighborhood groups (such as gangs and cliques), and fabricated groups (such as those formed by some

[3] Dimock, *op. cit.*, page 202. Association Press, 1937. Used by permission.

agency, e.g., the Church School, on the basis of age and grade).

The significant fact disclosed in this study is that the neighborhood or the natural group was found to be the most dominant factor in influencing and interesting boys from twelve to sixteen years of age. These groups were, in the very nature of the case, highly cohesive. On the other hand, most of the fabricated groups, such as those classes in a Church School department, were found to have a low friendship index [4] or a small degree of cohesiveness, and therefore a smaller amount of influence in a boy's life.

Wholesome Group Life Within the Church Setting

It is clear, then, from these studies that if the church is to influence the personality development of early adolescent boys and girls it must consider more seriously than ever before the strategic importance of natural groupings of these boys and girls within the church. It must face the task of making over mere collections of individuals (placed together because of age or grade) into cohesive groups in which there is a social life satisfying to adolescents.

There is need for more groups like the one in a certain rural church, where all the boys and girls of the community belong to the same Sunday School class, attend the same society meeting in the evening, and follow this with a jolly " sing " and refreshments in the different homes. The members of this same group often get together for parties, hikes, and for various

[4] By the term " friendship index " is meant the degree to which individuals in a group are real friends with the other individual members that make up the group.

projects which they carry out together. They have come to know each other intimately and find a great satisfaction in the co-operative enterprises they undertake.

There is need for more groups like the Holt family, who enjoy one another so much. Each member of the family has learned to play a different musical instrument and on long winter evenings they find it real fun to play together in their family orchestra. Each takes his turn at the housework. They plan surprises for one another and together plan family celebrations. They have indeed become a " co-operative commonwealth " in miniature.

The Christian Ideal for Group Life

Throughout its history Christianity, when most vital, has been characterized by that cohesive quality of group life called fellowship. The Christian religion was cradled in one of the most amazing fellowship groups conceivable, a band of twelve men, from diverse occupations and with varying temperaments and points of view, together with a Leader who had within him the genius for friendship. Out of these twelve men was fashioned an intimate group of associates characterized by comradeship — even though one of their members became a traitor. This band of disciples became the nucleus for the Christian fellowship we call the Early Christian Church — a fellowship which attracted the attention of the people of Jerusalem and later of the Roman world, who said of them, " See how these Christians love one another."

This band of disciples was the first great experiment in Christian group life — the nucleus of the Christian society which Jesus called the Kingdom of God on earth. Jesus not only taught certain principles of this Kingdom, but he sought to work them out in this group of men whom he chose as his close friends and associates. To them Jesus said, " Seek ye first his [God's] kingdom, and his righteousness."

The following characteristics marked this fellowship which he sought to build among men:

Love — genuine love for God, his Father and theirs, would be reflected in their relationships with each other as sons of God and brothers of each other. This love was to be sacrificial and self-forgetful.

The exalting and dignifying of human personality — each individual counting for something in his own right.

Democracy — whether rich or poor, slave or free, Jew or Gentile, young or old, wise or unlearned, all were to be treated with the same respect as children of God and therefore important in God's sight.

Co-operation — instead of competing with each other for places of advantage, they were to co-operate in the tasks of the Kingdom. One of their early leaders, Paul, likened their working relation to one another as similar to that of the different parts of the body, each one contributing its part and, therefore, important to the whole (I Cor., ch. 12).

Social responsibility — Christ enunciated the Golden Rule as the rule of the Kingdom, and Paul added, " If meat causeth my brother to stumble, I will eat no flesh for evermore." Voluntary denial of harmful things for the sake of a weaker brother was to mark this fellowship.

Spiritual before material values — and in this Christian fellowship recognition was to be given of spiritual values over material things. For Jesus once said, " A man's life consisteth not in the abundance of the things which he possesseth."

Such high ideals as these made up the concept of the Kingdom of God on earth for which Jesus taught his disciples to pray. In the relationships of such group life, and in intimate relations with their great Leader, there was to be found that abundant life which Jesus came to bring to men.

And the early Christians found in their group life joy and satisfaction. They became transformed personalities, forgetting their old limited selves with their cramping inhibitions in the satisfactions of belonging to such a group built around devotion to their great Leader.

Fellowship Groups in the Christian Church

Throughout the history of the Christian Church, since the early days, there have constantly been springing into being vital fellowship groups which exemplify in surprising fashion the principles of the Kingdom for which Jesus lived and died.

The monastic brotherhoods or communities in the Middle Ages may be considered of this character. The " Little Brothers of the Poor " originated by Saint Francis, the " Brothers of the Common Life," the Wesleyan class-meeting groups, and some modern groups today bear witness to the joy, the enhancement of personality, and the fulfillment of life which come from cohesive group fellowship in which there is a sincere attempt to carry out in everyday life the social principles of Jesus.

The United Christian Youth Movement

This ideal of a loving, democratic, co-operative, ethical, and spiritual society has been the dream of vital Christians in every century. This dream has also found concrete expression in certain social movements of our day which have helped to lift the level of corporate living higher.

Today the social gospel is being preached from many pulpits and an increasingly large number of Christian leaders are becoming more sensitive to its implications. " The Social Creed of the Churches," [5] formulated by representatives from the different Protestant Churches of America that make up the Federal Council of the Churches of Christ in America, has done much to raise the standard and to make people aware of certain unchristian practices in society which have been hitherto little challenged.

The Senior and Young People's groups,[6] through their United Christian Youth Movement, have become vitally interested in the enterprise of " Building a New World." But it is very doubtful whether young people will have the realistic interest in those social principles involved in the larger outreaches of this program if they have not already had some opportunity before they become Seniors to discover for themselves what it feels like to be members of such a co-operative Christian group, living out the relationships and the group life consistent with these social principles in a " miniature Christian community."

[5] From " Social Issues of the Churches," pages 1, 2. Federal Council of the Churches of Christ in America, 1933.

[6] It is agreed by most leaders of youth that Intermediates are too young to become a part of this program.

Living in an Unchristian Society

In the meanwhile, deeply entrenched in the corporate life of our country and the world are certain unchristian practices which hinder the realization of the Kingdom of God on earth. Perhaps most deeply entrenched of all is the competitive principle employed in our industrial and economic systems. This principle is to be found in the very fabric of local community life. It has crept into school systems, where methods of grading encourage and demand competition between pupils of varying degrees of intelligence, with the accompanying stress and strain which may endanger personality. It is sometimes to be found in local churches, with their emphasis on membership contests and memory drills.

Instead of true democracy, dictatorships seem to have become the popular mode in national life today. The darker races, subjugated and suppressed by the white race, are clamoring for their place in the sun. Clashes between white people and Negroes are frequent. Commonly observed also is the unjust treatment of minority groups; the conflict between capital and labor; and the misunderstanding and tension existing between the older and younger generations. Throughout the world, war threatens to destroy life's finest values. All this is in striking contrast to the spirit of love and democracy which Christ set as the pattern for a Christian society.

Mass production in industry and the development of a scientific knowledge of the universe have tended to make man seem insignificant as an individual unit. To the extent in which they have accomplished this

they have been unchristian. Many a boy growing to
manhood in this generation, if he succeeds in finding
any kind of employment, is apt to be forced into the
midst of an industry where for a livelihood he must
perform one single operation in the complex manufac-
turing of a motor car or some other commercial product.
He is unlikely, in his vocation, to have any adequate
opportunity for realizing the joys of creativity. He
will often be tempted to feel that the individual is not
after all important or significant in his own right but
only in proportion as he makes money for some concern
or for some man who is already too wealthy for his own
good.

He finds himself also in a world victimized by propaganda. Newspapers, billboards, radio, and the movies
will attempt to make up his mind for him. It will be
far easier for him to let them do it than to take the time
to ferret out the real truth for himself and to make his
own decisions. His thinking is, therefore, likely to be
dominated by the firms, agencies, or individuals with
large enough resources to control the channels of propaganda such as the radio and the press.

Still more serious, this youth of our generation will
grow up to take his place in a community and a world
in which spiritual values are largely eclipsed and ob-
scured by an abundance of material things. Success
will be apt to be measured by the extent of material
resources which he has at his command. A deplorable
example of this is to be found in the commercialization
of the Christian Christmas festival with its sacred
spiritual meanings. Too often the joy and value of
Christmas is measured by the number of things received.

Also, within the secularized school system, religion is often " pigeonholed " for a brief period on Sunday morning, and even this period for the cultivating of the religious life will be curtailed or eliminated from the schedule if parents allow other activities to crowd out the church and its program for youth. A confusion of values is very evident in modern life.

Christian Group Life in the Church

The clear, authoritative words of Jesus to his disciples in the first century, " Seek ye first his kingdom," remind us in no uncertain terms of the supreme goal of all our united efforts. Christian education leaders in co-operating Protestantism also remind us today of our major objective. They say, " The goal of Christian education is the Kingdom of God, a world in which God is recognized as the Father and all men act as brothers." [7]

Many religious leaders have become increasingly aware of the need for building a Christian world. Many sermons have been preached in an effort to arouse Christian men and women to their task of building the Kingdom of God in the world and in their community. But it is equally important that each local church shall examine its own corporate life to discover whether the principles of this same Kingdom are finding fullest expression there.

One recent writer says [8]:

[7] " The Organization and Administration of Christian Education in the Local Church." Book Six of The International Curriculum Guide, page 7. International Council of Religious Education, 1935. Used by permission.

[8] Johnson, Ernest F., " The Church and Society," page 94. The Abingdon Press, 1935. Used by permission.

" Only when the church has given effect to its social convictions by incorporating them into its own discipline has its address to the community any social reality."

And also:

" The most important social undertaking of the pulpit and of the Church School is to win acceptance on the part of the church itself of the principles of Christianity as expressed in social life — to bring the church *actual* nearer to the level of the church *ideal.*"

We might paraphrase the words of Jesus so that they read, " Seek ye first that kind of group life within the church which approximates Kingdom ideals, and all these other things — increase in membership, prestige, financial strength, and increase in influence in community — shall be added unto it."

Possibly one of the most significant ventures in connection with an Intermediate group would be to foster and develop groups within the church in which the social principles of Christianity would find full and complete expression. Then these same Intermediates might take their places later in the ongoing program of the United Christian Youth Movement with increased zeal and effectiveness because they have had the actual experience of participation in miniature Christian communities within the church, have found that joy and enhancement of personality which results, and are, therefore, more fully committed to the realization of such a Christian society in its larger outreach.

Some Implications

But what do we mean by a " miniature Christian community " in a Church School department? What will characterize group life for Intermediates within such a miniature Christian community?

1. The principle of democracy should prevail in the Church School department, or class, or club group. If group life within the church is to be thoroughly Christian, adult leaders should see to it that distinctions between the rich and the poor, the privileged and the underprivileged, the pupils with high intelligence quotients and those in the lower levels, and between the various racial groups, are minimized and that true democracy is promoted. The leadership should be sensitive to danger spots in the life of the group. Much can be done to avoid stress and strain. The highest type of social engineering will be needed to build within the Church School a sincere spirit of democracy. A fundamental element in this democratic spirit will be the kind of appreciation and understanding of the values which minority groups contribute. The development of this spirit in its farthest outreaches is a vital part of the program for world friendship or missionary education in the Church School.

Another factor in this democratic spirit will be the relationships which exist between the old and the young, between the more mature and the less experienced, between the different age groups in the church. More and more there should be built up a democratic relationship between teacher and pupil. More and more should pupils learn how to share the purposes of the leaders of a department or a class. There will also be opportunities for an exchange or interrelationship between the Beginners, Primary, and Junior departmental groups and the Intermediates, or between Intermediates and Seniors and Adults. It is important that younger adolescents shall feel themselves a part of the total church fellowship, sharing in the total church program and availing themselves of its benefits. At times, however, with this age, one of the most useful services of the leader of Intermediates will be to interpret them and their actions to those adults who are impatient with their awkwardness or overexpectant as to their abilities.

2. We shall also work toward the practice of cooperation instead of competition within departments, classes, and club or society groups. Consider what it would mean if every competitive device now used to increase membership, stimulate flagging interest, or accomplish other ends were to be replaced by a cooperative method in which boys and girls learn the satisfactions of working together toward worth-while goals instead of trying to defeat other individuals or classes or groups.

3. We shall also place special emphasis upon the intangible but nevertheless spiritual and social values, rather than upon material rewards which are outside the process itself. The most worth-while reward for work well done is a sense of belonging to a group and of having made a worth-while contribution toward furthering its enterprises. On this point Dr. William Heard Kilpatrick, the well-known teacher, says:

" In the degree that our young people seek any reward purely for the sake of the reward and think only of it and practice thus only selfish satisfactions, in that degree does the system of offering rewards build *not* moral character but selfishness. To use rewards and honors must be counted as immoral unless in fact the original satisfaction of the external reward . . . gives way to an inherent satisfaction in the activity itself or in the helpful effects of the activity. . . . At best they represent a mistrust in the power of the good life to afford real satisfaction and to win its own way." [9]

4. We shall also work constantly to build a feeling of group responsibility rather than individual effort. This would lead us toward group, rather than individual, projects wherever possible. These projects, however, should be of such a nature that the varying capabilities and interests of the individual members may be expressed in working them out. It will also mean that the leader himself should be careful not to assume responsibility which should be placed squarely on the group itself. Individual difficulties or behavior problems should be viewed, not in the light of the inconvenience they cause the adult leader, but in the results to the group of which the misbehaving individual is a part.

5. We shall also see to it that there are afforded genuine opportunities for each group member, as an individual, to express himself creatively in the way in which he is most capable, so that he may have the joy which comes from adding his own creative effort to the group enterprise. In this way the individual boy or girl may begin to feel his or her significance as a contributing member to society.

6. Since one great need of youth, growing up in the midst of propaganda, will be to discover the truth for himself, to weigh, to sift, and to judge it and then to act in the light of his best insights, we shall also give boys and girls opportunities to think, evaluate, and

[9] Quoted in Blair, W. Dyer, " The New Vacation Church School," pages 173, 174. Harper & Brothers, 1934. Used by permission.

discuss the various sides of questions so that they may learn how to make wise choices on the basis of the best knowledge at their command. This will mean a freedom and honesty between pupils and leader which will encourage a sincere interchange of thought.

7. Most important of all, we shall build toward that quality of cohesiveness within our groups in which there is an interweaving of friendship which turns a collection of individuals into a natural, friendly group with no one feeling an outsider, isolated from his associates. This will mean the cultivation of the art of making people feel at home, of manipulating situations so that the best side of boys and girls whose adjustment to others is defective may be expressed. It may sometimes mean that more attention will be paid to the desires of individual boys and girls to be in the class with their special friends and, perhaps, a little less attention to strict age or grade placement in groups. It will mean that a longer session, more frequent opportunities for the group to come together, and worth-while things for them to do together will be sought, so that in informal situations friendships can be developed and deepened.

The social ideals which have been suggested in this chapter will call for the most tactful, wise leadership. Those who attempt this leadership will need to keep constantly aware of the goals to be reached, but at the same time they will never be so engrossed in reaching these goals that they fail to use the most Christian and democratic processes in arriving at them. To think that one has reached a goal, only to discover that those whom one is seeking to lead are lagging far behind, or are scattered in every direction, is one of the great tragedies of an overenthusiastic leadership which fails to take into account the social nature of the Christian educational enterprise.

Will it not become one of the most challenging ventures of the Christian Church to build up groups of boys and girls so interrelated with larger groups that, both in the smaller and in the larger fellowship, they may experience the thrilling satisfaction of " belonging " to something worth-while, with work to do, standards to maintain, responsibilities to share? When these are merged into the larger fellowship of the local church and into the still larger fellowship of the Christian Church Universal, the Church will grow in strength and in vitality, through their loyalty and their share in it. And, best of all, personalities will be developed, abundance of life will come to the individuals involved, and the Kingdom of God on earth will be advanced.

Suggestions for Further Reading and Study

The most thought-provoking and helpful book will be Hedley S. Dimock's " Rediscovering the Adolescent." Read especially Chapters V, VI, IX, and X. Association Press, 1937.

For the social task of the Church read Ernest F. Johnson's " The Church and Society." The Abingdon Press, 1935.

CHAPTER III

BUILDING THE INTERMEDIATE DEPART-
MENT IN THE LOCAL CHURCH

HAVE you ever had the feeling that the program for boys and girls of Intermediate age in your church is without plan or purpose? Have you ever felt that the various leaders and the organizations appealing to boys and girls of junior high school age, within your local church, are working at cross-purposes or duplicating efforts? Or have you ever wondered whether your local church is really meeting the needs of the boys and girls in your church family as it should?

If you feel this way, jot down some of the special needs of Intermediates which you believe your church should meet. Spend some time evaluating your present program in all its aspects. Make a list of all organizations within your church which have anything to do with this age group. Find out what the objective of each of these organizations is, as it relates itself to the lives of boys and girls. How successfully is each of these organizations realizing its objectives?

Better still, meet with the other leaders of Intermediates in your church and discuss these important questions together. Look over the list of objectives given on page 47 of this chapter. Also acquaint yourselves with the statement of objectives for an Intermediate Department which your own denominational Board has suggested. Consult the statement of objectives given in your lesson courses and program materials. Determine, then, your specific aims for each department, class, society, or club group for the next few months ahead. Then, taking the Intermediates themselves into consideration, begin to plan a program of study and activity which you believe will help to meet their needs and to realize these objectives.

What Is a Program?

What associations does the word " program " bring to your mind? Do you immediately think of some special public occasion or of the various items on a radio program, instrumental selections, vocal numbers, dramatic skits? Or does the word bring to your mind the old-fashioned Children's Day or Christmas exercises, with the necessary preliminary rehearsals and practices? Or do you think of it in the way the term is commonly employed in Christian education today as a *plan of action*, a " blueprint " of what you hope to accomplish, ways of going about it, the tools with which to work, and plans for putting it into effect?

It may be defined in this way: " A program is a combination of all the methods and procedures for using curriculum materials, the experiences and activities of the boys and girls themselves, the experience and personality of the teacher, which are found useful in the guidance of pupils toward the realization of the goals which are set up." It is a " plan of action, including carefully formulated goals and the means of realizing them." [1]

[1] " Principles and Objectives of Christian Education," pages 84, 85. Book One of The International Curriculum Guide. International Council of Religious Education, 1932. Used by permission. Also Desjardins, Lucile, " The Pioneer Department of the Church," page 32. The Judson Press, 1936.

By the term " Intermediate Department " is meant the entire constituency of a given local church within the age range from twelve through fourteen years, or within the seventh, eighth, and ninth grades of the public school. The program includes the entire ministry of the church to boys and girls of these ages and grades in school. It includes not only the Sunday Church School program, but also the program of Scout troops (meeting in the church) ; missionary societies; evening society groups; Vacation Church Schools; junior church for this age; weekday classes; and classes in preparation for church membership.

A Builder Follows Certain Steps

Just as a carpenter would not think of starting to build a house by erecting the scaffolding before digging the foundation, so any group of leaders responsible for a program in a local church should follow certain steps of program-building: first, the architect's blueprint; then the foundation; then the scaffolding, the raising of the walls, and all the other various steps which a carpenter knows well must come in due order.

Wise leaders planning a program for an Intermediate Department will proceed in this way:

1. They will decide upon *general goals or objectives* for their program. These will compare with the architect's blueprint.

2. They will go to work to discover and study the interests, experiences, and needs of all Intermediate boys and girls within the local church. In the light of these they will formulate immediate or specific aims.

3. They will review the present program as now carried on in the local church and its effectiveness in

achieving these objectives and meeting these needs which have been discovered.

4. They will gather and review program suggestions. At this point it would be a good idea to take the boys and girls into consultation.

5. They will determine what resources are available for the program in the way of materials and equipment, and will try to think of ways and means of adding to these what is necessary.

6. They will determine the leadership available and will make an effort to secure adequate leadership.

7. They will locate, centralize, and distribute responsibility.

8. They will set to work to put the program into effect, making whatever adjustments are necessary as they proceed.

9. They will judge of the effectiveness of the program at intervals.

10. As a result of their thoughtful evaluation, they will make whatever changes are found necessary and desirable in the achieving of the goals.

The process of building the program is thus a continuous one, with constant adjustments to meet changing needs.

This present chapter will deal with the first three of these steps of program-building. Other steps will be dealt with in the following chapters.

Adequate Christian Goals

Some church groups exist and " carry on " after a fashion, merely because it is the accepted thing to do and because the minister and the church expect them to do so. The lack of a true sense of direction in their teaching on the part of some Church School leaders reminds one of the conversation Alice had with the Cheshire Cat, in Lewis Carroll's whimsical tale:

" ' Will you please tell me which way I ought to walk from here? '

" ' That depends a good deal on where you want to get to,' said the Cat.

" ' I don't much care where,' said Alice.

" ' Then it doesn't matter which way you walk,' said the Cat.

" ' . . . so long as I get somewhere,' Alice added as an explanation.

" ' Oh, you're sure to do that,' said the Cat, ' if you only walk long enough.' " [2]

It is important for leaders to ask themselves at intervals such questions as: " Why am I teaching in the Church School? " or " What do I sincerely hope to see realized in the lives of these boys and girls in this department and in the ongoing program of the church through my efforts and through the efforts of those working with me in this department? " and " Is our program based on custom and tradition or on an intelligent recognition of the needs of growing persons? "

The Wise Men of old followed the star until they came to the place " where the young child was." We of today need to share their wisdom by having an adequate goal for our efforts, one which will give power and significance to our everyday tasks. Dr. Henry Wieman, in " The Issues of Life," [3] says that every person needs the " Bethlehem star " of a great purpose, if life is to be lived at its very best. So too does

[2] Carroll, Lewis, " Alice in Wonderland," page 55. E. P. Dutton & Co., Inc., 1929. Used by permission.

[3] Wieman, Henry, " The Issues of Life." The Abingdon Press, 1930.

a department or a class need leadership with a clear-cut, adequate purpose if it is to accomplish worthy results in the lives of its pupils. Furthermore, Dr. Wieman says that we all need to expose ourselves to the power of this sovereign purpose on frequent occasions if its power is to make our lives more effective. So too the leadership in a Church School needs to expose itself frequently to the power of a great purpose if the department is to continue to function effectively.

In some ways the recital of a great purpose at stated times may be more useful to us than the recital of the Credo in a Sunday morning church service, for a statement of a goal or purpose is functional. If really meant, it gives direction to activities, it determines our selection of means and of materials, it becomes a measuring rod by which we may measure the results of our educational efforts.

The Goals of Christian Education

Co-operating Protestantism has formulated seven major ultimate objectives which indicate the direction in which the Christian education program of the local church should move.[4] These objectives were arrived at by a consensus of opinion of leading religious educators throughout the country and have formed the basis for the curriculums and the programs of the co-operating denominations. Like the star which the Wise Men followed, they point the way toward the realization of the divine dream for Christian personality and for a Christian society.

[4] "Principles and Objectives of Christian Education," pages 10–17, *passim*. Book One of The International Curriculum Guide. International Council of Religious Education, 1932. Used by permission.

They are briefly as follows:

1. To lead growing persons into an understanding and appreciation of the personality, life, and teaching of Jesus Christ.

2. To foster in growing persons a consciousness of God as a reality in human experience and a sense of personal relationship with him.

3. To foster in growing persons a progressive and continuous development of Christlike character.

4. To develop in growing persons the ability and disposition to participate in and contribute constructively to the building of a social order embodying the ideal of the fatherhood of God and the brotherhood of man.

5. To lead growing persons to build a life philosophy on the basis of a Christian interpretation of life and the universe.

6. To develop in growing persons the ability and disposition to participate in the organized society of Christians — the Church.

7. To effect in growing persons the assimilation of the best religious experience of the race, as effective guidance to present experience.

Objectives for an Intermediate Department [5]

While the objectives given above apply to every age, nevertheless there may be particular points of emphasis at different stages in the development of childhood and youth.

Certain of the denominations have formulated their own statements of goals for the Intermediate Department, based upon these seven objectives. The following statement has been adopted by the Presbyterian Church in the United States of America and by the Northern Baptist Convention for their Pioneer Department programs [6]:

[5] Write to your own denominational Board for the objectives recommended for an Intermediate Department.

[6] Desjardins, Lucile, "The Pioneer Department of the Church," page 6. The Judson Press, 1936.

The desired outcome of Christian education in the individual is a growing Christian personality. The development of this growing Christian personality in Intermediates involves:

1. A growing realization of God as Father; a developing faith in his unique power, infallible wisdom, and perfect love; and a growing sense of friendship with him.

2. A definite and voluntary personal acceptance of Jesus Christ as Saviour, Lord, Friend, and Example; a growing appreciation of his life, work, and leadership; an increasing commitment to his way of life.

3. An appreciation of the Bible as a guide for Christian living; an increasing knowledge of its content and skill in its use; appropriation of those values in literature, art, and life which offer further guidance for Christian living.

4. A definite effort to live as a Christian in all life situations, particularly those that involve the increasing desire for independence and self-expression, the making of choices, and questions of adult authority.

5. Sympathetic appreciation of the inherent values and possibilities in all peoples, a growing fellowship with all who are striving for the Christian ideal, and the manifestation of Christian attitudes toward class and social distinctions.

6. Intelligent membership in the Christian Church and willing acceptance of and preparation for individual responsibility in its program.

7. The acceptance of a share of the responsibility of presenting Jesus Christ to all men everywhere; and a growing concern for the attainment of the Christian ideal of universal brotherhood and social righteousness and suitable participation in the effort to attain this goal.

The Methodist Episcopal Church, South, through its General Board of Education, has set up the following departmental objectives for Intermediates:

To help all young people to achieve a vital relationship with Jesus Christ as personal Saviour and Lord.

To help all young people to grow in Christian character.

To help all young people to render effective and joyous service to the world. [7]

Immediate Aims — Specific Objectives

The ultimate aims are like the far-off sunrise toward which we lift our eyes; immediate aims are like the steeple of a certain church which marks the end of one stage of our journey. Ultimate aims are like the star which guided the Wise Men over desert and fertile land and river; immediate objectives are like the oasis which they hoped to reach by nightfall.

Ultimate objectives depend upon the message and purpose of the Christian religion, revealed in the New Testament writings; immediate objectives are a part of the daily life situations of individual pupils as the goals which they wish or need to achieve. Specific, immediate objectives are concrete and sharply defined. They are practical, as, for instance, to help John and Mary to learn how to get along without quarreling all the time. They can be determined only as the leader comes to know intimately and well the pupils whom he is teaching.

For example, in a certain church in a combined Intermediate and Junior Department there seemed to be a lack of respect and attention during the opening service of worship. Apparently standards for work and study were also low in that department. Such an attitude made it clear to the leaders that the church itself did not rate very high in the estimation of this

[7] Brown, Elizabeth, "Intermediate Department Handbook," page 6. General Board of Christian Education, Methodist Episcopal Church, South, Nashville, Tennessee, 1936. Used by permission.

group. However, a gift of a certain amount of money to this church made possible the reconstruction of the big barren-looking departmental room into an attractive chapel, with separate study rooms on each side. With this added equipment and with a special need in mind, the group of leaders set to work to see what they could do to build up in the minds of these boys and girls an attitude of respect for the church, a feeling for real worship, and a work attitude in connection with the Church School. They looked through their lesson material for the coming quarter, made selection of points for special emphasis, and planned projects and other procedures which would accomplish these desired ends. Their specific purposes, which lay within the area of number 6 of the ultimate objectives (see page 47), influenced and decided their particular procedures.

In some cases, specific objectives might be determined by questions members of the group are asking, indicating mental confusion and eagerness for help in certain philosophical or religious areas. In other cases, the need might be that of helping them in certain conduct problems which have arisen; or some particular emphasis in the public school might call for a supplementing of information and a religious interpretation in the Church School program.

In deciding upon these immediate aims it is important not only to recognize the group needs and interests; it is wise also to recognize the needs of individuals within the group, for each is a distinct personality and may require a different type of guidance. Especially is the range of interests great within an Intermediate group. These varied interests need to be taken into consideration.

In the midst of this process of formulating aims, leaders must also bear in mind the total church program and be aware of what has already been stressed in the Primary and Junior Departments and of what will probably be stressed as these pupils pass into the Senior and Young People's Departments. Wise indeed is the leader who can select with true discernment the needs and the interests of growing youth which, because of their crucial importance, shall be made the center of a church program.

Leaders need to realize the importance of building on what has gone before. Continuity is necessary in a Church School department. This continuity will insure to a child who grows up through the different departments the help in all the areas of life where he needs help. Throughout the church program there should be some architectural plan as the pupils progress from department to department. To make this certain it is a wise plan for leaders responsible for different age groups to meet together and share in outlining their programs, thus getting a bird's-eye view of the total curriculum and program of activities. Thus will they obtain a more complete vision of the " mosaic of their common task."

Determining the Needs and Interests of the Group

It is evident that a leader or group of leaders cannot proceed to determine specific objectives without discovering the needs, interests, and experiences of the boys and girls for whom the church has responsibility.

Some attention has been given to this matter in Chapter I. It is enough to say here that an increasing number of techniques have been developed within the past few years for discovering the attitudes, the concepts, the skill in moral discrimination, and the information possessed by growing persons. This is because the experiences of growing persons are taking an increasingly important place in all educational planning.

There are various approaches to the task of getting at the underlying attitudes and basic needs of this age group. One approach is through the study of the environmental factors influencing the life of boys and girls within the community. Such an approach would lead one to the study of the curriculum and program of the public school; the analysis of the program of Boy Scouts, Girl Scouts, and other character-building agencies; a study of the movie situation in the community, and of other community influences which have to do with the life of boys and girls.

Another approach is through the use of tests to discover, for example, the amount of correct Biblical and other religious information possessed by individual members of the group. One may also discover through tests the attitudes and the ability to discriminate between right and wrong possessed by different boys and girls.

Very often certain glaring needs will become apparent through conduct problems which arise within a department or class. Or, in a class discussion, some question may arise which may seem to be much more vital and crucial than those considered in the lesson materials being studied at the time.

The use of an interest finder may uncover certain areas that are of more vital interest to the group than others.

Another essential approach is through conferences with parents to obtain their reactions and their points of view, as well as their feeling of the importance of certain needs to be met in the lives of their growing boys and girls.

The thoughtful filling out of the following chart [8] may be another helpful approach to determining the needs on which a church program for Intermediates may be built. In order to use this to the best advantage it would be an excellent plan to invite for consultation the representatives of other community agencies. They would then be able to give information as to the areas of experience particularly stressed by the agencies they represent. For example, determine what agency is doing the most in the way of a health program. Does the public school carry on an adequate program in this area? Or do the homes of the church constituency care for this aspect of the life of the boys and girls? Follow along down the line, discussing each area and checking it. The specialized religious area (the last one in the column) will naturally be considered the special duty of the church and the home. But it may be that neither public school and community organizations nor homes are adequately providing wholesome recreational life for this age. In that case the church should seriously consider what it can do to supply this need or to stimulate community leaders to make up this lack.

Wherever one of these areas is being neglected for

[8] Found in "How a Leader Proceeds with a Group," page 21. Pamphlet Number Two of Christian Quest Series. International Council of Religious Education, 1927. (Out of print.) Used by permission.

Areas of Experience	Where Touched				Needs
	Home	School	Club	Church	
Health.					
Education.					
Economic life.					
Vocation.					
Citizenship.					
Recreational life.					
Preparation for marriage, parenthood, family life.					
General group life.					
Friendships.					
Aesthetic area.					
Specialized religious activities.					

this age group, the different agencies should determine which of them is best prepared to undertake its enrichment. Such a careful study should also avoid duplication of effort within certain areas of life experience.

Reviewing the Effectiveness of the Present Program

In the light of the discovered needs and the objectives which have been formulated, the present program should next come under careful scrutiny. Every phase of the church program for junior high school boys and girls should be carefully studied and evaluated. This would include the entire ministry of the church to this age group. It would include: Church School department and classes; society groups; expanded pe-

riods; Vacation Church School; Weekday Church
School classes; confirmation groups or pastor's classes
preparing for church membership; the church service
of worship as it affects boys and girls of this age; Boy
Scout and Girl Scout troops; and mission bands or societies.

Certain questions should be asked regarding this
total program:

1. Is it realizing the goals of Christian education?
Is it leaving unrealized certain important objectives?
Is there a conflict of purposes?

2. Does this program take into account the real
needs and interests of the boys and girls to whom it is
attempting to minister? Compare the list of interests
and needs in connection with Chapter I. How many
of these is it failing to take into account?

3. In this program is a balance maintained between
adult and pupil leadership? Is there evidence of
democratic participation in the program? If not, it
is failing in one of the most important aspects of
Christian group life.

It is sometimes temptingly easy for adult leaders
who have surveyed the interests and needs of their
pupils to assume entire command of the situation and
attempt to force upon the group the program which
they have determined will be the best for the pupils,
since they feel that it has been scientifically arrived at.
But the ideas of the boys and girls themselves should be
taken into consideration. At this age they are interested in having a share in planning for a departmental program. To be sure, adult leaders will find
pupils of this age sometimes lacking in experience and
in dependability. But herein lies a need which cannot

be ministered to by an adult assuming the command. The solution is not adult domination but, rather, co-operative efforts between adult leaders and youth. The leaders of Intermediates should conceive their job to be that of preparing boys and girls to take upon their shoulders an increasing amount of responsibility. Committees for various responsibilities should be chosen and given a chance to function. Perhaps one of the most useful services a leader can contribute at this stage of development, when boys and girls are learning the art of leadership, is to act as a stopgap between them and the misunderstanding of overexpectant adults. Leaders in this department should measure their success, not by the artistry and finish of the projects undertaken, but by the extent to which boys and girls increasingly share in the purposing and planning and in the increased skill with which they carry through enterprises with a minimum of adult initiative.

4. Are the motivations social and Christian?

In the program of Christianity, which lays such stress upon the inner spirit with which a man serves and the inner attitude he possesses, it is especially important that the form of incentive used should· be carefully studied, for the motives with which one undertakes a task have a profound influence upon the personality growth of the individual. Very many worth-while enterprises have been carried forward to a successful conclusion within a church which have appealed to comparatively low and selfish forms of motivation for their success. Attendance is often stimulated for a period in certain Church Schools by competitive contests or by the offering of prizes. Much

more effective in the end than such extrinsic forms of
motivation is the kind of wholesome interest generated
through seeing to it that there is a genuine democratic
participation in the making of program plans. Where
there is active, purposeful participation, there is almost sure to be increasing interest, and where there is
genuine interest in the program plans themselves, there
is no need to resort to more artificial incentives.

5. Is the program comprehensive? Does it seek to
meet all the needs of the junior high school age group
which it is the part of your local church to meet? Has
this program been planned with the entire community
program in mind?

6. Is the program unified? Is it a total program for
the church as a whole? Do the pupils feel themselves
a definite part of the entire church program? Is it
unified within itself, each part having a definite relation to the whole?

7. Is the program well-balanced? Or are certain
features overstressed and others minimized? Is it
strong on Bible study and weak in recreational and
social life? Does the Scout program overtop every-
thing else in the mind of members of the department?
Do they come to Church School so that they can have
a share in the athletic games during the week?

8. Does the program provide variety enough in its
activities so that those who have differing interests
and abilities may find opportunities to participate and
to make a creative contribution?

9. Is the program flexible? Or is it so rigid that it
has got into a rut and does not make allowance for the
shifting interests and needs of this younger adolescent
age group?

When you have answered these questions satisfactorily, then you will be ready to set to work to build the foundation for an effective program. Your next question will be, What in the old program should be abandoned or changed, and what should be retained? You will then wish to turn your attention to other important considerations, such as the elements which should enter into this program, the materials or tools which you will wish to use, and adequate leadership to carry it forward.

For Further Reading and Study

Brown, Elizabeth, "Intermediate Department Handbook," Guidebook for Adult Leaders. General Board of Christian Education, Methodist Episcopal Church, South, Nashville, Tennessee, 1936.

Carrier, Blanche, "How Shall I Learn to Teach Religion?" Chapter 4. Harper & Brothers, 1931.

Desjardins, Lucile, "The Pioneer Department of the Church," Chapter 3. The Judson Press, 1936.

Fiske, George W., "Purpose in Teaching Religion." The Abingdon Press, 1927.

McKibben, Frank M., "Intermediate Method in the Church School," Part II. The Abingdon Press, 1926.

Smith, Robert Seneca, "New Trails for the Christian Teacher." Chapter 4, "Importance of Aims in Christian Education." The Westminster Press, 1934.

"A Manual for Leaders of Intermediates," pages 17–23. Christian Board of Publication, St. Louis, Missouri, 1937.

"Church Work with Young People of Junior High School Age," Guiding Principles for a Program. Division of Christian Education, Board of Home Missions, Congregational and Christian Churches, Boston, Massachusetts, 1938.

"Pioneers on Kingdom Trails." The Manual. The Young People's Division, Executive Committee of Religious Education and Publication, Presbyterian Church, U. S., Richmond, Virginia.

CHAPTER IV

ESSENTIAL ELEMENTS IN THE PROGRAM

A CARPENTER builds his house out of wood or stone or brick. What are the essential elements out of which an Intermediate Department program should be built? This is a puzzling question to many people. Someone will say:

" When I started to Sunday School years ago, all we did was to study the Bible and to learn the answers to the questions in the Catechism. But young folks do all sorts of things in the church now that I never dreamed of doing when I was a girl."

This leader is right. The program of the church for its children and young people has grown amazingly within the last fifty or seventy-five years. In fact, there is almost as much difference to be found between church programs then and now as there is in the little red schoolhouse of a century ago — teaching only the three R's of education: reading, 'riting, and 'rithmetic — and the modern, well-equipped junior high school, with its provision for courses in physical education, home economics, manual training, music, and vocational guidance.

Today, in modern Church Schools, worship, missionary education, recreational and social activities, discussions on personal and social problems, and service projects are all considered essential elements in a complete and adequate program of Christian education.

They find their place along with a study of the Bible and of the great beliefs of the Church.

Not only has the program widened to include in its scope extra-Biblical materials. It has also widened the range of activities considered suitable and effective in teaching religion to boys and girls. In an adequate program today, boys and girls learn how to worship together, to play together, to do worth-while things together for others, to search for information, to investigate, to study, and to discuss the facts they have discovered. Suggestions for all these are included as a very definite part of most denominational curriculum and program materials.

Bearing in mind this contrast between the old and the new, turn again to your present program for Intermediates. Ask these questions:

1. What *study courses* have been used recently in the Church School sessions on Sunday morning and in the other groups meeting in the evening or during the week? What has been the major emphasis in each? Check the following:

  a. Biblical content._____
  b. Church history or beliefs._____
  c. Religious biographical study._____
  d. Missionary education._____
  e. Discussion of personal or social problems._____
  f._____

Are the boys and girls growing in their understanding of the religious life, the Bible, the Christian Church and its world-wide service program? _____

2. What *service projects* have been carried through successfully during the past few years?

a. For the local church._____
b. For the community._____
c. For national or home missions._____
d. For foreign missions._____
e. Dramatic projects._____
f. Exhibits._____
g. Visiting, planning programs for other groups._____
h. Constructive projects of other kinds._____

3. What *recreational* or *social activities* have been carried on this past year? _____ How helpful do you consider them in developing a wholesome group spirit? What problems, if any, arose in connection with these social occasions? What is being done to make use of or develop hobbies or special leisure-time interests?

4. What is being done to develop attitudes of *worship?* Are the worship services carefully planned? rich in content? appealing to the members of your group? What is their attitude during worship services? What opportunities are given boys and girls for training in the leadership of group worship? What informal worship experiences have the boys and girls been having in class or society or informal groups? What has been done to help them to develop habits of daily private devotions?

5. What opportunities for the study and use of *symbolism* and *ceremonials* are afforded the Intermediates in your church?

6. What special efforts are made to lead boys and girls to an intelligent decision for Christ and the commitment of their lives to him? Are these efforts made at special times in the church year, or are they made consistently throughout the year, whenever the opportunity arises? What opportunities are given for train-

ing in preparation for church membership? What opportunities for studying the program of the church and for participating in the program?

7. In what way is *missionary education* being cared for in your church for this age group? What training is given in *stewardship* and in the financial aspects of the church program?

If you have any questions or doubts concerning the advisability of including recreation, missions, evangelism, or service activities in an Intermediate program, discuss your questions or doubts with other leaders of your department or church or leadership education class.

In a vital and adequate program there will be the interweaving of study, discussion, activity, fellowship, and worship elements. Good times together, doing worth-while things for others, searching for truth and gaining information, looking to God for inspiration and guidance — these will all have their place in a forward-looking program for junior high school youth; for we must never forget that this generation of boys and girls will someday be the adult worshipers in the church. They will be the ones to pass on to a new generation of the young the accumulated religious knowledge of the past. The church must also depend upon them to carry forward its local and world-wide service program. And they must begin early to prepare themselves for these responsibilities.

The Place of Study in the Church School Program

Real, purposeful study should have a vital place in the Church School program for youth. Any activity or enterprise in the carrying out of which there is not a continuous demand for investigation, for learning new things, for enriching one's background with the religious heritage of the race, for acquiring new meanings, may be considered of doubtful value for a program of Christian education. But it should be *study with a purpose* — not only for the leader but for the pupils themselves. Missions, modern problems, biography, hymnology, history, and especially the Bible should all be objects of study, not as ends in themselves but to enrich life and further social purposes. The desire for study or investigation should, if possible, arise out of a felt need for further information in order to achieve some purpose real to the boy or girl. The forced study of a Sunday School lesson, when the need for what it contains has not been made apparent, does not yield so large a return in vital learning as does the study which takes place voluntarily on the part of those who wish to do their share in furthering a class project and need the information to accomplish this.

In many cases all the individuals of a class group will not be studying the same materials. One person or a committee may be working on a report to give to a class, while another group may be investigating another aspect of the problem. Further suggestions concerning the study element in the program will be given in connection with Chapter VI, which deals with class procedures.

Projects in the Church School

Within recent years, Church School leaders have been learning that through the carrying out of worthwhile projects boys and girls discover how to study purposefully and achieve many values for Christian personality development. The following are examples of enterprises which, under efficient leadership, have value in the Christian educational program of the local church.

A club of Intermediate girls [1] in the First Baptist Church of Newton Center, Massachusetts, was especially interested in India. The girls wanted to give a play. When they were asked such questions as: What do you know about India? about its people? its religions? its customs? the discussions showed the poverty of their knowledge. (A good starting point for purposeful learning.) They readily saw the need of some study as a preparation for their play. They listed the topics about which they felt the need for further information, and divided their group into committees for investigation and report. Two weeks were spent on these reports. The girls wrote to their denominational offices for specific information and were thrilled to receive " real business letters " in reply. All this helped to give the proper atmosphere for beginning the play. From a number of possibilities they chose to present " Piyari's Rescue."

As they proceeded they found new difficulties — how to pronounce Indian names, how to drape saris, and so forth, and again investigation was necessary. They went as committees to those who knew and secured their information; and thus the play was finished.

Then they wanted to share their experiences with the church. Their pastor agreed to let them have a Friday church night for the purpose. They made

[1] Reported from Missionary Education Bulletin, World Fellowship. Division of Christian Education, Congregational and Christian Churches, Autumn, 1930. Used by permission.

attractive programs of blue construction paper, cut in the shape of the map of India, to which was attached a white sheet with the program and cast of characters. In addition to the play there was an exhibit of the club's work — a scrapbook containing pictures and a record of what they had done, cretonne school bags made for the boys and girls of an Indian orphanage, and a diminutive stage representing the scene of the play, with dolls dressed in Indian saris. As a part of the evening program the whole project was explained by one of the leaders. She showed that the project was really the girls' own. That was the secret of their enthusiasm and the reason why the whole experience was so vital.

It is evident that this project measured up to the following tests of a project of real Christian educational value:

1. The choosing and the carrying out of the project was democratically done — not imposed on the group by a teacher or leader.

2. So far as appears in the description, the carrying out of the project was done in a Christian way so that each girl had a chance to learn how to work with a group in a Christian way.

3. The group felt that the enterprise was significant as a church and a Kingdom enterprise.

4. In the carrying out of the project much useful information was acquired purposefully, in line with the content of a Christian educational program.

5. The project was completed with a satisfactory culmination in which the members of the group had an opportunity to share with others the results of their efforts.

6. It is to be hoped that the members of the group evaluated their project at the close, discovering points of strength and weakness, and were, therefore, the better prepared to launch forth on some other enterprise for the church.

The Intermediates in a Wisconsin church were interested in learning the story of how the Bible has come down to us from the past. The members of one committee decided to make a large combined mural and time chart which would cover one wall of their departmental room. On a yard-wide strip of tough Manila paper, they began to sketch a road. This road represented the trail of the centuries. Along this road they drew pictures to represent certain incidents and characters in the Bible story which they felt were most important. At the extreme right of their time chart and mural, at the point which represented the twentieth century, they drew the picture of an open Bible. But still they were not satisfied. So below this picture they drew one of a boy and a girl reading an open Bible. But they were not yet satisfied. Finally, after much thought and discussion, they decided what should be their third and final picture, representing the influence of the Bible in the lives of people. They drew the picture of a colored and a white person shaking hands with each other.

It is apparent that back of this enterprise, guiding and helping to give meaning to their activities, was an effective leader who helped the committee to see the values and the religious meanings in the things they were attempting to do.[2]

[2] For other projects, consult " Things to Do for the Junior High School Age." Activities and resource material. Division

Many possible projects will suggest themselves to a resourceful teacher if they are not already suggested within the curriculum and program materials being used. Making a relief map of Palestine, gathering together old and interesting copies of the Scripture for a Bible exhibit, forming art galleries of pictures of the life of Jesus by different artists, making pilgrimages or visits to churches and community institutions, planning group notebooks — are all possibilities which have educational values in the hands of the right leader. But these guided group activities should be an integral part of the ongoing program, and not extraneous activities "tacked on" to divert attention from the real issues. Whatever project has been selected, it should be the means of helping the group to enter more purposefully into the entire department and church program. It should result in real "learnings" important in a Christian educational program and in the building up of that kind of Christian fellowship in the group which we are seeking to achieve. The boys and girls should feel that through this thing which they have achieved by co-operative effort they have really advanced the cause of the Kingdom and of the church.

Recreational and Social Activities

Any leader who has struggled along with a group of uproarious boys or indifferent, giggly, and bored girls knows what magic is sometimes accomplished by a simple, informal get-together in one's own home or at

of Home Missions of the Congregational and Christian Churches, Boston, Massachusetts. See also "Projects for Intermediates in the Church Program." Intermediate Work Department of Epworth League and Young People's Work, Methodist Episcopal Church, 740 Rush Street, Chicago, Illinois.

a campfire party out in the open. Such occasions are often the beginning of intimate, informal, happy group associations, which are so influential for growing adolescent personalities. They furnish bewildered leaders a more intimate insight into the real persons they see sitting before them on Sunday morning. They also furnish the chances boys and girls need to learn the social techniques so essential for their later social life.

Hedley Dimock says [3]:

"What the adolescent does when he is free to do what he likes is of weighty consequence for the present and the future. In his play pursuits, his resources as an adult for the use or the misuse of the gift of expanding leisure, forced upon him by the machine, are in the making. In the experiences of play, the deepest needs of his personality may be wholesomely satisfied or tragically thwarted. Through the subtle and pervasive influence of those with whom he intimately associates in play, his social attitudes, standards, and conduct are being inescapably patterned."

And also:

"Play interests and behavior are central, rather than peripheral, then, in the development of the adolescent. They possess possibilities that are pertinent to his education for leisure, the satisfaction of his basic personality needs and desires, the formation of his social attitudes and habits, and the revitalizing of contemporary education."

If we neglect the rich social and religious values wrapped up in such social and recreational occasions so that boys and girls fail to find within the church program the sense of joy, mastery, success, and achievement which comes from belonging to a worthy social group, contributing to its welfare, and partici-

[3] Dimock, Hedley S., " Rediscovering the Adolescent," page 33. Association Press, 1937. Used by permission.

pating in its program, they are very apt to fall back on the programs of entertainment and physical activity provided by commercial agencies, which are not always planned with personality needs in mind.

Mr. Dimock also suggests the following criteria of an effective education for leisure for adolescent boys, which might also be applied to girls:

" 1. The interests or activities engaged in should be capable of persisting on the adult level. . . .

" 2. There should be a distribution of play or leisure pursuits among activities that in their predominant characteristics are physical, intellectual, aesthetic, and social. This does not imply a balance among these types of activities since individual variations in interests, aptitudes, and abilities should be recognized, discovered, and definitely encouraged. But he whose resources for living are undeveloped and barren in any of these trunk lines of recreational activity is missing some rich sources of satisfying experience.

" 3. Some of the leisure pursuits of the individual should be active, some self-propelled, and some creative. . . .

" 4. Some of the interests of the persons involved should be primarily social and others essentially individual." [4]

Worship in the Pioneer Department

One of the central elements in any program for the junior high school age is worship. Worship should do the following for Pioneers:

1. It should open the avenues of approach to God through prayer, Bible study, music, beauty, nature, art, literature, and personality.

2. It should bring a fuller realization of the worth and pre-eminence of spiritual values in life.

3. It should help to achieve a life purpose, so that all choices may be made in harmony with that purpose.

[4] *Ibid.,* pages 58, 59.

4. It should bring sensitiveness to the needs of their fellow men and help in creating devotion to the program of the Kingdom of God on earth.

5. It should provide experiences which prove valuable as training in private devotional life.[5]

Some departmental superintendents and general superintendents, especially those who are faced with the need for a combined worship service group made up of Intermediates, Seniors, Young People, and Adults, are in despair because of the apparent indifference, inattention, and disorderliness shown on Sunday morning during the opening period for worship. On the other hand, this period set aside for group worship holds within itself the deepest and richest possibilities for creating religious attitudes and binding individuals together into a vital group fellowship.

If there is difficulty in this phase of the program a most careful analysis of every phase should be made, including the setting for worship, plans for preparing the service, its content, the participation or lack of opportunity for participation in it by the group, the group's reactions to it, and the personality of the leader. One secret of solving the problem is through more democratic participation in the planning and carrying out of the service on the part of the boys and girls themselves. This gives the group a sense of belonging which brings with it a special interest and a feeling of responsibility. If a worship committee is chosen for this, an adult counselor will be needed who understands how to counsel without dictating. The

[5] Brown, Elizabeth, "Intermediate Department Handbook," page 12. General Board of Christian Education, Methodist Episcopal Church, South, 1936.

problem of centering about a theme is somewhat more difficult when the groups within a department are studying different lesson units than when they are all centering on one emphasis at the same time as is the case when Group Graded or Departmental Graded materials are being used. But this difficulty can be overcome by building up an interest in the possibility of each group's sharing with other class groups the most interesting and valuable things it has been studying.

Where the Intermediates are forced, because of lack of room, to share a worship service with older or younger groups, care should be taken that the elements in the service are neither too juvenile for them nor too much above their level of interest and comprehension. It is often wise to pass around the responsibility for planning this service so that Intermediate class groups may have an opportunity to prepare the worship service and then to lead the rest in the service which they have prepared.

Symbolism and Ceremonials

Experienced leaders know how interested some boys and girls become in symbols and ceremonial observances. The obscure and cryptic elements in some ceremonials appeal to them. It is fun to have a secret that they can keep within their own group and share with only a favored few in an initiation service. Ceremonials, expressing certain great truths in a formal way through a series of carefully arranged symbolic acts, have a strong appeal to adolescent boys and girls, who enjoy a certain amount of formality once in a while, especially when they have a share in creating the form and are on the inside as to its secret meaning.

Several of the denominations have capitalized this interest in the developing of club programs with initiation ceremonies and progress from one rank to another. The Camp Fire Girls, the Boy Scouts, and the Girl Scouts make use of this ritualistic element also. So also do summer camp programs for this age group.

The following principles [6] should guide a leader in making use of ceremonials:

1. They should be dignified and formal.

2. They should be beautiful in form and appeal to the aesthetic as well as the religious.

3. The setting should be carefully planned, chairs arranged in an effective way, and all symbols used with the greatest respect.

4. They should not be used too frequently, but reserved for special occasions.

5. There should be careful preparation down to the minutest details. Matters of exact formation, the precise way each participant is to contribute, should be carefully planned beforehand. Special attention should be given to a plan for concluding the ceremonial and dismissing the group.

6. They should not be too long, so that participants have to stand in one position for too long a period.

A study of the symbols in the church will prove fascinating to some Intermediates. Through these symbols

[6] Adapted from pages 51, 52, Lucile Desjardins, " The Pioneer Department of the Church." The Judson Press, 1936. See also those in " Handbook for Leaders of Pioneer Boys (or Girls) in the Christian Quest," pages 109 ff. The Westminster Press, 1930. Suggestions from mimeographed paper, " Enriching Group Life Through Ceremonials." Committee on Religious Education of Youth, International Council of Religious Education (1934–1935).

they may come to understand something of the interesting history which lies back of the Church and some of the important things for which the Church has stood in the past.

Evangelism and Church Membership

In the past, many churches have depended for their emphasis on evangelism — on certain revivalists coming into the church from outside at certain seasons of the year to hold special meetings in which a certain amount of enthusiasm is stirred up and feelings of guilt aroused on the part of those adults and young people outside the church fold. While some churches still continue the practice of periodic revival effort, many people are beginning to feel that such spasmodic efforts are not permanent in their results and, because of their overemotional appeal, sometimes prove harmful rather than constructive in their effects on adolescent personality.

In other churches the confirmation class is an established part of the church program in preparing boys and girls for church membership. Chapter VII will deal with this phase of Christian education.

Missionary Education and Stewardship

Many denominations have ceased to encourage separate mission bands and other missionary organizations for young people and children. They are emphasizing the fact that Christian missions are an integral part of the total church program, for they are really the logical expression of Christian principles and Christian attitudes in relation to those who may be outside one's own immediate locality. Missionary-minded women of these denominations are, therefore, directing their energies to seeing to it that the missionary emphasis and the study of Christian missions are made a definite part of the Church School program on Sunday morning, in the evening society programs, and in the weekly sessions. The mission boards of these denominations are planning their programs in co-operation with the church boards of education, so that the regular Church School curriculum materials contain definite missionary emphasis and content. The stewardship emphasis is also found in most age group materials and in the programs sent out by denominational boards, and is being made an integral part of church programs with special times and seasons when it receives particular emphasis throughout the local church.

Suggestions for Further Reading and Study

See discussion of program areas in Elizabeth Brown, "Intermediate Department Handbook," pages 11 ff. General Board of Christian Education, Methodist Episcopal Church, South, Nashville, Tennessee, 1936.

Also, "What Types of Activity Should Be Included in the Program?" pages 7–15, "Church Work with Young People of Junior High School Age." Division of Christian Education, Board of Home Missions, Congregational and Christian Churches, Boston, Massachusetts, 1938.

McKibben, Frank M., "Intermediate Method in the Church School," Chapter 5. The Abingdon Press, 1926.

For specialized elements:

Harbin, E. O., "Recreational Materials and Methods." Cokesbury Press, 1931.

Kerschner, Mabel, "Missionary Education of Intermediates." Friendship Press, 1929.

Shaver, E. L., "The Project Principle in Religious Education." The University of Chicago Press, 1924.

"International Standards for Intermediate, Senior, and Young People's Departments." International Council of Religious Education, Chicago, Illinois, 1930.

Chapter V

MATERIALS FOR THE INTERMEDIATE
DEPARTMENT

Have you ever been perplexed and wondered where you could find materials which would be suitable and interesting for your Intermediate Society group? Or for your Vacation Church School department? Or for your Sunday Church School class? Or for departmental worship services? You will probably find others in your community who are facing the same difficulty.

If you are studying this textbook in an interdenominational leadership training school, why not, as a special class project, arrange an exhibit of all available Intermediate materials which are being used in your local churches, including Sunday School lesson quarterlies, elective units, story papers, society topics quarterlies, missionary education textbooks, Weekday Church School courses, and Vacation Church School courses. Add to these worship materials any other supplementary source materials which help to enrich your local church programs. To this display of denominational and interdenominational materials you might also add Boy Scout and Girl Scout, Camp Fire Girls, and Four-H Club handbooks. Write to your denominational board for help in this. They will send you prospectuses and, perhaps, samples of material you may not be familiar with. Arrange all these in an attractive display and plan a time when Intermediate workers may have an opportunity to examine the various books and pamphlets. You will discover what an abundance of material is available for our work with younger adolescents. This means that there is all the greater need for selecting with care what you will use to carry forward and enrich your program.

Lesson Courses Available

On display you will probably find at least four or five different varieties of Sunday Church School lesson courses which are used in different Church Schools. There will be:

International Uniform Lessons.

Group or Departmental Graded Lessons.

Closely Graded Lessons.

Elective Courses.

Indigenous Courses (prepared independently by local church).

Write in the space below, the type (or types) of lessons and the publisher (or publishers) of the courses which Intermediate groups in your local church are using at present. If you are not clear as to the difference between these, turn to pages 86–91 in this chapter for further explanation.

My local church is using for Intermediates:

Name or Names of Courses   Types of Courses   Publishers

Selecting Materials

Whatever the program planned for Intermediates, there will certainly be need for some printed materials. If such resources are not available, the leaders will be badly handicapped in carrying their plans forward. But various practices prevail when it comes to the selection and use of these materials.

In some local churches lesson materials are largely prescribed by custom and tradition. They are ordered as a routine matter, by some official in the church or Church School, from the denominational supply house, and the teachers use them lesson by lesson without taking into consideration the immediate needs and interests arising within the group which, at times, may call for the use of a different type of lesson material than that prescribed. The effectiveness of their use in a local situation will depend partly upon the skill and the resourcefulness of the local leader, and partly upon the extent to which these materials have been planned with this particular age group in mind.

In still other departmental groups the leaders have " thrown overboard " courses of study and are using whatever their whims and fancies may dictate. Sometimes these leaders have a very limited knowledge of what is really available in the field of curriculum for this age group. Some of them reject or ignore the available materials which have been carefully worked out by denominational leaders, and reach out for certain nondenominational materials published by private and commercial concerns, because they promise to be cheaper or easier to use, or because they seem more in line with their own particular adult theological

views. The result of such a haphazard selection is that
a program of study grows up like " Topsy " — without
sequence and balance, and sadly skewed in emphasis.
An excellent illustration of this practice is found in
those classes which have decided to read the Bible
through, chapter by chapter, with the help of certain
juvenile Bible storybooks. While they are reading the
Old Testament through, whole areas are being omitted
from their study and their thinking. Then too such
departments are apt to find themselves in the predica-
ment of one Intermediate Department in which the individual teachers discovered too late that each one
had decided to teach a course on the life of Paul while
other rich areas for study and discussion were left untouched.

In the third type of church the lesson materials are
chosen on the basis of the needs and the interests of the
age group, and in accordance with objectives which
have been formulated for the departmental program.
Care is taken that the materials chosen provide sequence and balance, so that they furnish a well-
rounded, cumulative curriculum based squarely upon
a Christian philosophy of life and education. They
see to it that the curriculum for the junior high school
department is well articulated with the program for
the Junior Department and with the Senior Department program. These leaders are well aware of the
range and the variety of materials which their own denominational board makes available to them. They
are conscious of the fact that most denominational
lesson material has back of it the co-operative study
and investigation of all the denominations represented
in the International Council of Religious Education.

They are aware of sources to which they may turn for materials to supplement their own denominational units when a special need arises. They have learned how to evaluate many types of lesson material and to make an intelligent selection on the basis of certain criteria. If they are in doubt, they are ready to accept the judgment of their own denominational age-group leaders whose advise they gladly welcome.

Criteria for the Selection of Lesson Materials

The following questions [1] should be asked before the final selection of any lesson materials for use in an Intermediate Department or class:

1. Is the point of view expressed in this material consistent with a Christian philosophy of life? Will it help in the realization of the objectives of Christian education?

2. Will this material definitely help to realize the specific goals formulated for the local department or class?

3. Are the educational procedures described or implied in the teachers' and pupils' books in accordance with the best thinking in the fields of public and religious education today? Do they imply a traditional or a creative approach to teaching?

4. Is the pupils' material suited to their interests, and the vocabulary and content within range of their understanding?

5. Is the literary form and structure of the pupils' material equal, at least, to that of literature recommended for use in the public school they attend or by the library from which they are accustomed to draw books for reading?

6. Is the mechanical form of the pupils' material attractive? Is it well printed? attractively illustrated?

7. Have the materials been selected with due regard to the principles of sequence, unity, balance, and comprehensiveness when viewed in relation to the total program?

8. Will these materials supply patterns for action which will stimulate boys and girls to live noble Christian lives?

[1] Desjardins, Lucile, "The Pioneer Department of the Church," pages 59, 60. The Judson Press, 1936.

A Unit of Work

The term " unit of work " used so frequently in place of older terms such as " courses of study " may seem confusing to some. It really means: " A number of worth-while experiences bound together around some central theme of pupil interest and need."

Sometimes a pupils' quarterly may contain the description of more than one unit of work, with the materials and procedures built around more than one central theme or problem or project. For example, a quarterly may contain two units, one on " The Church " and another on " The Bible in Mission Lands Today."

The following principles governing the selection of units in the Church School program have been formulated by a Weekday Church School committee.[2] They are also helpful in a general discussion of curriculum-planning.

1. The curriculum should include units dealing with all significant experiences of growing persons.

2. The curriculum should contain units which contribute to the realization of each of the major goals of Christian nurture.

3. There should be a sufficient variety of units within the field of each trunk-line experience and within the field of each major objective to provide for adequate guidance for each child.

4. Units should be selected for each age group which take account of fruitful interests and of needs that are likely to be dominant during that stage.

5. It should be recognized that there can be no hard-and-fast division of units among age groups, as such groupings are varia-

[2] " Selecting and Using Curriculum Materials in the Weekday Church School," Service Bulletin No. 620, page 10. International Council of Religious Education, 1937. Used by permission.

ble from community to community. Units which will be used in the third grade in one community may be used in the second grade in another, and in the fourth grade in still another.

6. The selection of units should take into account the degree of skill on the part of the leader and the amount of resource material required, such as books, pictures, outside leaders.

How to Adapt and Supplement Program Units

Sometimes the question is raised: How may we use the printed material supplied by our denominational publishing house and at the same time build a program suited to the special needs of our local church and department and class?

The answer to this question is to be found in the process of adapting and supplementing with which creative teachers are familiar.

Sometimes teachers who fail to understand this process ask: " How can I ever use all the material given in my quarterly for one class session? I can't possibly cover it."

Most of the new units are planned and written with much more material included in them than could possibly be used in a class period. This affords the resourceful teacher a chance for choice.

Suggestions for this process of adaptation and enrichment are to be found on pages 15 and 16 of Bulletin 620.[3] The general outline is as follows:

1. Read the entire unit through carefully, discovering its purpose, desired outcomes, the experiences upon which it is built, possible activities as a means of sharing this needed experience in Christian living, its source materials, its organization, and its practicability in suggested sessions, the relation of sessions to the entire unit, and so forth.

[3] See page 91.

2. Read the unit through again with one's own situation and group in mind, taking account of such considerations as these:

(a) Does this unit deal with experiences which are vital needs to members of the group?

(b) Would they be interested in this plan of study?

(c) Are they capable of such a study? Have the pupils' school and other educational experiences prepared them to follow the educational approach and methods used in this unit?

(d) Have the pupils pursued any such study in public school, Sunday Church School, or in any other character-building groups? If so, is there any unique and needed guidance which our class experience should share in completing this experience? How can the work done in this field be correlated so that there will not be duplication or serious omission?

(e) Is this unit most useful at this season or at another season?

(f) Are activities proposed such as can be carried out at this season?

(g) Is it desirable to give the number of sessions required for this unit in view of other needed guided experiences?

(h) Is there time enough before the end of the year for this unit?

(i) Are the space, equipment, supplies, funds, class enrollment such as to make possible the successful use of this unit?

(j) Is the leadership available capable of using this unit successfully?

(k) Are sufficient source materials supplied?

(l) Are the source materials usable in one's own situation and group?

3. A detailed plan for using the unit:

(a) Build a specific purpose for one's own work with one's own group.

(b) List some specific desired outcomes if this purpose is fulfilled.

(c) List the best and most possible activities for the group.

(d) List the best available source materials to be used in this particular study.

(1) Those provided within the unit.

(2) Those available in public and church libraries.

(3) Community resources.

(e) Chart the course on paper for one's own group, making columns as follows: purpose, outcomes, activities, source materials, and so forth.

(f) Plan out possible stimulating environment or ways of setting the stage for initiating such a unit of guided experience in one's own group.

(g) Plan on paper carefully the first session, having in mind the pupils, their needs and interests in this field.

(h) Decide on the probable number of sessions necessary for an adequate guided experience in the field of this unit.

(i) Outline the rest of the unit as you see it now by sessions.

(j) Reread the plans and replan the sessions after every session with the group, making careful plans for the new session.

(k) Keep a narrative report of each session. The following outline is suggested for it: the situation out of which the activity arose; what the boys and girls purposed to do; how the boys and girls and teacher planned together, giving description of the enterprises; the Christian outcomes.

(1) What knowledge have the pupils acquired?

(2) What habits have they seemed to form?

(3) What attitudes have they seemed to develop?

(4) What leads into new interests and new needs have been revealed?

It is an excellent plan for a department or class leader to file copies of all quarterlies or units or periodicals and to keep in scrapbooks or in folders all supplementary materials which might later prove useful. This would apply not only to materials for the Sunday Church School session but also to worship materials for the departmental program and discussion materials for the evening society meeting. What would be useful to the pupils could then be brought out and placed on a browsing table when needed in the development of a new unit.

Whether all the class groups of a department are

using the same units or different ones there will be need
for the class projects and work to be integrated, so that
each will contribute to a larger departmental enterprise if departmental loyalty and consciousness are to
be built up.

It is an excellent plan for a departmental superintendent to call for a conference of his teaching staff a
month or several weeks before the beginning of a new
quarter or before the class groups start on new units.
When Group Graded, or even Uniform materials, are
being used the leaders can come prepared to discuss
and to plan for the introduction of the new unit in their
various classes. They can plan together for possible
departmental projects growing out of the unit. In the
large Church Schools where Closely Graded materials
are being used, the departmental group might divide
into committees for a preliminary session and then
bring back reports to the rest as to possible plans for
their individual classes.

The stated objectives for each unit should be placed
on the blackboard and considered thoughtfully in the
light of the local situation and the experiences and
needs of the local group. In the light of these, specific
aims and desired outcomes fitted to the local group
should be formulated. These should be written down
and carefully studied.

Projects or enterprises which the department as a
whole, or class groups, might be interested in undertaking should be discussed. Each teacher may have
in mind several interesting activities from which members of his class might choose one to carry out.

Procedures involved in using the new unit should
be considered. If the teachers feel that they lack skill

in some of these techniques, books or chapters from books on methods may be referred to and suggested for reading; or someone versed in these particular methods may be invited to the conference to give help; or the teacher may be encouraged to observe some other leader who is skillful in the particular procedure required.

Supplies necessary for the development of the unit should be listed, along with source materials which would help to enrich it. A collection of books and other source materials might be gathered into a library for both pupils and teachers.

Plans for initiating the unit should also be discussed. It is often desirable to give a pretest of some sort, which will uncover gaps in knowledge or any lacks which this particular unit is designed to fill. A test may also be given at the end of the unit to discover what improvement has been made in these particular matters during the time covered by the unit.

Sometimes the introduction of a new unit will mean the shifting of the equipment in order to make possible procedures that are different from those formerly used. For example, it may be that the working out of a certain unit may call for wall space for murals or time charts or posters. Or it may call for cases or exhibit tables where an exhibit or collection may be displayed.

It is a good plan for the teachers and departmental superintendent to find out from the public school anything the pupils have been studying that would tie up with the unit to be started in Church School. For example, in one town the Vacation Church School planned and carried through a unit on Palestinian life, only to discover in the midst of it that the State Teach-

ers' College Experimental School, which some of the
pupils attended, had just previously developed a similar unit with the same pupils, under much better conditions and with superior facilities for work.

Description of Available Program Materials

There are many types of lesson materials, suited to
different purposes, which various denominational
agencies are publishing. To be reckoned with also are
nondenominational materials designed for this age,
published by private concerns.

1. *Sunday School lesson courses.* There are three
general types among these. The oldest, in point of
origin and in point of educational theory involved, is
the *International Uniform Lesson Series.* These lessons are planned primarily for those above Junior age.
They were started on the supposition that it is a most
excellent practice for everybody in the Church School
to be studying an identical Bible passage on the same
Sunday. The International Uniform Lesson Committee has had a long and honorable history, having
started on its work as far back as 1872. This committee plans a six-year cycle of lesson passages designed to cover the Bible. They alternate from the
Old to the New Testament. Accompanying each lesson passage is a Golden Text to be memorized. The
outlines planned by this interdenominational committee are released to the various denominations which
make up the International Council of Religious Education. Lesson writers then plan and write lesson
helps adapted to the various age groups. It is apparent, however, that a Biblical passage which might be
most helpful and inspiring to an adult, or even to a

high school student, or to a college student, might not be of great interest or even of great value to a child or a growing boy or girl of junior high school age, with special needs clamoring for attention. Most of the denominational publishing houses publish *Improved Uniform* lessons for Intermediates. Many Church Schools, especially the smaller, one-room and two-room schools, still use them. Samples of these lessons may be obtained from your own publishing house.

Some denominations publish *Group Graded* or *Departmental Graded Lesson Materials*. A committee from the International Council of Religious Education prepares outlines for Group Graded lessons also. Those committed to the Group Graded plan use the same theme and basic lesson passage for all those within one department. Several denominations use these International Council outlines, when feasible, and revise them when necessary to meet their own denominational need. Some prepare their own Departmental Graded outlines.

This type of lessons, it is evident, is a step forward from the Uniform lessons. They are especially adapted for smaller Church Schools, where there may not be more than one or two classes to a department. The added fact that they afford an opportunity for developing projects and building worship services around a central theme for a department commends them to many larger churches also. The pupils' material for Group Graded lessons is published in most cases in quarterly form for Intermediates. The teachers' helps are usually given in the various Church School journals published by the denominations.

Another type of material, the *Closely Graded Les-*

sons, follows the practice of grading in the public school, each separate grade having different courses. In this plan the pupils advance from year to year to new courses, with no two grades studying the same lessons at the same time. While it is evident that these lessons are particularly adapted for the larger Sunday Schools, where departments are organized with a separate class for each school grade, nevertheless some smaller schools use them by combining all the seventh-, eighth-, and ninth-grade pupils in one class and studying the seventh-grade material the first year, the eighth-grade material the second year, and the ninth-grade material the third year of the cycle. Several of the denominations publish their own Closely Graded series. Among these are the Bethany Graded Series, the Keystone Graded Series, and the Christian Nurture Series. Several denominational groups unite in publishing theirs under a syndicate called The Graded Press.

Some nondenominational courses are based on the International Uniform lesson outlines. Others follow a Group or Closely Graded plan.

One may also secure from the various denominational publishing houses helpful elective courses adapted to special situations and special groups.

2. *Society materials.* Some of the denominations follow the plan of printing their helps for society meetings in their story papers, which are distributed on Sunday morning. Others follow the Christian Endeavor topics published by this organization in The Christian Endeavor World, supplemented by a little booklet giving a few simple notes. Still others publish their society helps in a form similar to the Sunday School

quarterly. Some denominations have official youth publications in which society topics appear as, for example, in The Epworth Highroad. The Methodist Episcopal Church Board of Education has a series of undated elective units which may be used in evening groups. They are called " Everyday Adventures in Living Series." Some of these are planned with Intermediates in mind. In addition to these, some denominations have very helpful elective units which may be used for discussion groups.

3. *Story papers.* Most denominations supply story papers for Intermediates. Some nondenominational publishers supply story papers also, designed for Church School distribution.

4. *Program-building guides.* Many of the denominations publish program-building guides, such as the following:

Brown, Elizabeth. " Intermediate Department Handbook." General Board of Christian Education, Methodist Episcopal Church, South, Nashville, Tennessee.

" A Manual for Leaders of Intermediates." Christian Board of Publication, St. Louis, Missouri, 1937.

Desjardins, Lucile, " The Pioneer Department of the Church." The Judson Press, 1936.

" Pioneers on Kingdom Trails." The Manual. The Young People's Division, Executive Committee of Religious Education and Publication, Presbyterian Church, U. S., Richmond, Virginia.

" Church Work with Young People of Junior High School Age." Division of Christian Education, Board of Home Missions, Congregational and Christian Churches, Boston, Massachusetts, 1938.

Several denominations have also developed Pioneer club programs.

5. *Co-operative Vacation Church School texts*.
There has been developed interdenominationally a se-
ries of texts for use in Beginners, Primary, Junior, and
Intermediate Departments of the Vacation Church
School. The Co-operative texts for Intermediates are:

"Discovering God in the Beautiful," by Nathana Clyde.
The Judson Press, 1934.

"We All Need Each Other," by Mary Jenness. Methodist
Book Concern, 1935.

"Our Living Church," by Lucile Desjardins. The Westminster Press, 1936.

A list of available material for the Vacation Church
School program may be found in Service Bulletin No.
803 (revised), "Available Materials for the Vacation
Church School."

The Weekday Church School curriculum is in a
somewhat chaotic state. In past years the Abingdon
Series, published by the Abingdon Press, held the field,
with several miscellaneous texts which grew out of the
Weekday Church School experience in certain communities.

The Abingdon Press is now publishing a new series
of texts, designed primarily for the Weekday Church
School situation but used for various purposes. They
are called "Guides to Christian Living," and are edited
by Paul Vieth. They are planned on the basis of a
two-year span, with two texts designed for the seventh
and eighth grades and two for grades nine and ten.

The Weekday Professional Advisory Section, acting
jointly with the Committee of Religious Education of
Youth of the International Council, have been doing
some experimental work in the development of units
in certain local situations. The recently published

Service Bulletin, No. 620, " Selecting and Using Curriculum Materials in the Weekday Church School," lists available material for this type of school.

Besides all those described above, each denominational headquarters has a variety of pamphlets, books, and other helps which are recommended especially for Intermediate group leaders. These may be secured by sending directly to your own publishers.

Another type of material useful in the complete program for Intermediates is that published by the Friendship Press in the field of missionary education. Each year there are two current themes or emphases, one for the homeland and one for the foreign field. A leaflet giving the current Intermediate units may be obtained from the Missionary Education Headquarters at 150 Fifth Avenue, New York City.

Helpful plans for departmental worship services, with poems, prayers, suggested hymns, and stories, built around certain themes, are printed each month in the International Journal of Religious Education, 203 North Wabash Avenue, Chicago, Illinois.

A detailed list of materials for courses on church membership is to be found on page 134 in connection with Chapter VII.

For each unit also a teacher will be able to obtain help gleaned from here and there — from libraries, from one's own reading, from the pastor's library, and from books which may be purchased at a reasonable price — which will enrich the unit. These materials may be placed on a browsing table, in a special library nook, or tacked up on a bulletin board for the use of the pupils.

As you begin to accumulate useful materials for your

Intermediate program you will doubtless be faced with the problem of what to do with them when they are not in use and how to file them away so that you will know where to lay your hands upon them when they are needed. You should have a definite system for this. Large Manila envelopes are handy for pamphlets. Articles, poems, and other worship material clipped from magazines may be pasted on cards of uniform size and their subject or theme plainly marked on them and then filed away. A small card catalogue is useful in which to file away cards listing the various types of materials you have accumulated and where each is to be located.

It is evident that it would be an endless task to print within the covers of one textbook all the titles of all the available books and pamphlets of forty or more Protestant denominations. Therefore, it will be necessary for you to get in touch with your own denominational boards and publishers to see what they recommend for your use to help you in your particular situation. The International Council of Religious Education has compiled a bibliography of Intermediate courses in a mimeographed edition called "Available Materials for Intermediates." This lists courses by denominations, describes them briefly, and gives the objectives or areas in which they lie. It may be obtained from the International Council Headquarters, 203 North Wabash Avenue, Chicago, Illinois.

Chapter VI

PROCEDURES WITHIN THE CLASS OR CLUB GROUP

Have you ever felt that your class or your society group might be bored because you usually do things the same way every Sunday? To tell the honest truth, have you sometimes been slightly bored yourself because there seems to be so little chance for variety in procedures?

But there are, really, a great many ways to go about this business of teaching younger adolescents. Just to test yourself, look through the list below and check those you have used in your Sunday Church School class or your society or missionary group within the last two months. Add any other methods you have used and place two checks before the ones you felt were most effective in accomplishing your objectives.

Procedures I Have Used Within the Last Two Months

Group discussion.	( )
Lecture method.	( )
Use of a check list or test.	( )
Storytelling.	( )
Group planning.	( )
Use of pictures or other visual aids.	( )
Silent reading.	( )
_____.	( )

Write down, or describe orally, as accurately and objectively as you can, just what took place in your group during the last session you had with it. How did you proceed and what did the members of your

group do in response? If you feel dissatisfied with
your teaching, get someone to come in and, without
gaining too much attention, take down in shorthand a
verbatim report of your class session some day. Study
this verbatim report carefully to discover how your
procedures might have been improved.

How Learning Takes Place

The basic educational unit in the Church School is
the class, or club, or society group. Here teachers and
pupils meet from Sunday to Sunday or during the week
and, as a result, either desirable or undesirable learning takes place. But whatever learning results from
the situation, you may be sure it is because certain
fundamental laws are in operation which are deeply
rooted in human nature.

Mr. G was discouraged about his class. He seemed
to get nowhere with it. A few Sundays before, the
boys had been all set to discuss certain items in a code
of ethics for an athletic team. There had been a base-
ball game between their school and a near-by rival
school. Several controversial issues had arisen. The
boys were not at all sure what was the right thing to
do in several of these issues. But Mr. G did not even
take into consideration the boys' keen interest in this
matter. He tried to get them started in the Old Testament lesson for the day, which happened to be on the
career of King Saul. The boys were not particularly
interested in King Saul or in any of the Hebrew kings
— they had lived too long ago. So while Mr. G talked,
the boys wriggled and twisted. A question or two
brought little response. Some of them listened politely
to what he had to say. Others tried to attract the at-

tention of the girls in the next class. Some made
" smart answers," which drew a laugh from the rest.
No wonder Mr. G was discouraged. The boys' response to this situation was by no means new. They
were accustomed to acting in this way. Phil had been
in a different class and was shocked at first by the way
the other fellows acted. But he wants to be on good
terms with them and he likes to gain their approval
by his smart remarks, so the habit of " wisecracking "
in the class has been growing on him.

Mr. L's class responds quite differently. Mr. L understands what boys are thinking about and are interested in. On the same Sunday described above, the
boys in his class were soon in the midst of an earnest
discussion of the right and wrong of certain athletic
practices. They listed these practices on the blackboard. Then they turned to their Bibles to see if they
could discover any principles to guide them. Before
they were through with their class session they had
associated in their minds some of the reasons why the
big, strong, " athletic " fellow, Saul, failed as a leader
and some of the reasons why boys and men fail today.
The boys were all set also to study the lives of other
Old Testament characters to see what they had in
common with modern leaders. But the most important
" learning " which the boys received was that Church
School is concerned with the way a fellow plays the
game and lives his life every day. The boys had such
a good time discussing things together that they were
ready for future study and were thus building up desirable habits and attitudes.

This second teacher was aware of the fact that the
boys in his group were *ready to act* in either one direc-

tion or another. He knew that the psychological *law of readiness* works on Sunday as well as during the week. He knew that according to this law the things his group might say or do would be the result of his skillful guidance or, on the other hand, they might be their reaction against his violation of this law or attempt to dominate the situation regardless of their interest. Mr. G violated this law of readiness and was suffering the consequences.

In Mr. L's class, the discussion on a vital issue was such a satisfying experience that the boys wished to repeat it. In Mr. G's class Phil found his satisfaction in wisecracking. Both were responding to another basic law of learning, namely, that when individuals have acted or responded in a certain way and have found the results satisfying to themselves, they will be much more apt to act in the same way again than if the act were accompanied by unsatisfactory results. This is called the *law of effect*.

Another law comes into operation here, namely, that when individuals repeat certain responses several times there will be a tendency to act in the same way again. This is known as the *law of exercise*.

With these three fundamental laws of learning the teacher in the Church School must reckon. Working in harmony with these laws, learning proceeds in the direction of the desired goals. Working in violation of them will certainly result in failure to realize these goals.

A Happy Relationship Between Teacher and Pupils

One of the very first things a new teacher should do is to establish a happy, friendly relationship with the group he is to lead, for the atmosphere of the class-room, or the " class corner," or the " class pew," is very important. This friendly relationship must be built upon understanding and insight. Getting to know a group involves certain very definite procedures. So the new teacher or the old teacher meeting a new class for the first time will probably need to have

An Introductory or Exploratory Session

The purpose of this kind of session is to get acquainted with the pupils, to discover their interests, to understand their problems, to realize their felt needs and their limitations, to become aware of their points of view and their attitudes, in order to lay a solid foundation for further vital teaching and learning.

One rather young teacher of Intermediate girls once remarked in a Leadership Education class:

" Oh, I always let my girls talk first about anything they like, and then — I give them the lesson."

If teaching is really guidance, then this sort of free interchange of experience, in informal fashion, lies very close to the heart of the teaching process. It is not something marginal. If the teacher is aware of his opportunity and skillful in guiding this conversation, he may help the members of the group to catch the significance of experiences which they have perhaps considered trivial. He may help them to discover alternative ways of choosing and behaving and he may also help them to evaluate the choices they have made according to a higher, more Christian standard.

This exploratory session may be carried on through informal conversation alone, through conversation supplemented by use of a blackboard, or through the use of simple check lists and interest finders.

Miss A felt the need of using this kind of procedure before she began to teach a unit on the Bible and its history. She planned an informal conversation around such questions as these: " What is the first idea which pops into your head when somebody says the word *Bible* to you? " and " What are some of the questions you have sometimes wished you might ask about the Bible? "

The teacher should be sure to encourage free and frank discussion. Nonshockability is an essential item in the teacher's attitude for these exploratory sessions and, in fact, for all discussion periods. While, at the first, pupils may try out a new teacher, presenting ideas which are alien to their own ways of thinking just to test him, if a teacher treats with seriousness and respect the ideas of the group he will usually find the pupils responding with like seriousness and honesty.

Initiating a Project or a New Unit

Mrs. B wished to start a new missionary unit on the Near East and the denominational missionary program there. She wished to interest the members of her group in this study so that they would enter into it purposefully and with a real zest. So on the Sunday that they were to start the new unit she arranged her corner of the departmental room with pictures which a missionary friend had sent to her from Iran. On the inside of the screen which separated her class from the others she placed several news items about events taking place in the Near East. She arranged on the table several well-illustrated books from the library, some of them opened to interesting pictures showing customs in the Near East.

When the first members of the class arrived, they started looking at the pictures, their curiosity was aroused, and they began to ask questions about Iran and other countries of the Near East. This teacher was skillful enough not to attempt to answer at once all the various questions which were asked, even if she had been able to do so. Instead, one member of the class was chosen to write down all the questions on the blackboard for future reference. Before they knew it, under her skillful guidance, they were beginning to plan among themselves things they might do to share with others the knowledge about these countries which they were now eager to acquire. They were also trying to think of the best thing they might do to help forward the missionary program in Iran. The plans proposed by the various members of the group were all written down by the secretary for still further consideration. By the end of this first class session, the members of the group were thoroughly interested in finding out something about Iran and Christian missions there. They also had a number of ideas of things they might do from which to choose. And they were aware of a number of interesting books and pamphlets which would be useful in gaining their information and in helping them to carry out their projects. Mrs. B felt that her objectives for that class hour had been achieved.

Miss D wanted to get a Bible unit off to a good start. She found in the library some books with colored plates of illuminated manuscripts made by the monks of the

Middle Ages. Another book produced a picture of a monk at work copying a manuscript. In another book she found the story of how one of the rarest of all manuscripts had been discovered in a convent on Mount Sinai when a traveler stooped to examine the contents of a wastepaper basket. In her pastor's library she found several of the newer translations of the Bible, including Moffatt's and Goodspeed's. All these she arranged on the table in the small classroom used by the group. Examining one of these after the other, members of the group soon began to ask questions. These questions were written on the blackboard. Before the class session was over, each person had agreed to find what facts he could about the Bible during the week. Without any special pressure on the part of the teacher, the members of the group found themselves launched on a study of " How We Got Our Bible."

A Period for Group Planning

Once any unit is introduced and enthusiasm for it aroused, the most natural question which follows is, What can we do about it?

This means one of two things, depending upon whether a democratic or a dictatorial procedure is to be used. If a dictatorial procedure is to be used, of course the teacher will have to plan every detail of the project in advance. But the very genius of an educational project lies in the pupil purposing which goes on in connection with it. Therefore, although the teacher may have several ideas " up his sleeve," so to speak, the group should have plenty of chance to suggest interesting things to do. One of the next steps, therefore, after interest and curiosity have been aroused, will be to make a list of tentative projects that the members of the group might like to carry out in connection with this unit. The number and the difficulty of the things proposed as well as the time limitations and the facilities available for work must be honestly faced.

List on the blackboard all the ideas suggested by the group. Consider together the feasibility and practicality of each of these, so that the members of the group will be aware of certain limitations from the outset. Find out from them resources or abilities they may have which would influence the choice of one enterprise in preference to others. Then, in the light of all these considerations, have them decide the things they might undertake and for which they would be responsible.

Certain responsibilities should then be distributed either to committees within the class or club, or to individuals if the group is small. Plans for the next week's work should also be considered. Each person involved should have a clear idea of his own responsibility. If he accepts any responsibility he should be held to it, not by the teacher alone, but by the group itself. Under such conditions, a member of the group will be far more likely to carry on his part outside the class than if this were an assignment made by a teacher to an individual pupil. Make sure also that books and other resources necessary are available, and that the individuals involved have definite ideas about how to proceed, so that some measure of success may result. In this way, experiences in carrying forward a part of a project are likely to be more satisfactory and, therefore, likely to be repeated.

Helping a Group to Become Aware of a Need

In some cases the adult leader or counselor may be quite aware of a need, but the boys and girls themselves may be quite unaware of it. In such a case the teaching procedure would be somewhat different.

Mr. H found this to be true with his class of boys. They came in one day quite hilarious about a trick they had played on David, a Jewish boy in their room in school. It appeared from their conversation that such tricks were the custom rather than the exception in their school. There was only one Jewish boy in their room, and he was evidently having a tough time of it. The class was in the midst of a unit on the life of Jesus. Mr. H did some thorough study during the week. The next Sunday he told them the story of the Jewish people (concealing the name of the nationality) leading up to the climax in the life of Jesus and then went on to mention briefly such outstanding members of the Jewish race as Julius Rosenwald, Albert Einstein, and Felix Mendelssohn. He referred also to the plight of the Jews in Germany. By this time the boys were thoroughly interested and, though the name of David had not once been mentioned, one of the boys volunteered that perhaps David might like to come some Sunday and tell about modern education in the synagogue. This was the beginning of an entirely new idea of the life of Jesus, with special emphasis upon the Jewish background of his life and the Jewish background of lads growing up in American cities today. And David no longer was the butt of their jokes.

Other ways of helping groups to become aware of problems and needs not now within range of their consciousness are: visits to special places, case stories to discuss, bringing in of resource leaders.

Discussion of Conduct Problems or of Religious and Philosophical Problems

Often in the very midst of a unit there arises a need for discussing some conduct problem which has arisen, or of facing together a religious perplexity which some individual member in the group may bring up on his own initiative.

For example, Mr. H was asked by the departmental superintendent to bring up in his class the fact that the boys in going to and from their classroom were disturbing the Primary Department and were sometimes rough in jostling their way through, so that the smaller children felt timid about going through the hall. Such questions as these call for a free and frank facing of the problem, even though the unit under way is neglected for the time being. One method the teacher may use, if there is a president or a chairman of the class, is to ask this person to bring up the matter. The problem should be explicitly stated from all its many angles. Any excuses the class members may have or points on their side should be brought out. Various ways of responding may be discussed and placed on the blackboard, and suggestions for action listed. There should be nothing of the scolding attitude on the part of teacher or leader. The thing should be faced quite objectively and every effort should be made to bring out not only a sense of responsibility to their own group to maintain their standing, but also a feeling of responsibility for the conduct of the whole school and for the welfare of the Primary Department. The group might even suggest that the members be made a traffic squad to see that the younger children have a clear right of way in the halls. If the teacher is on good terms with the group, there will be none of the attitude, in conduct problems, that the gang must stick by their comrade at the expense of the total situation. Pupil and teacher will act together. On no account should the teacher appeal to the group on the basis of his personal reputation or feelings. It should be clearly a matter of the group and group responsibility.

Committee Work and Reports to the Group

Very often plans are made in the entire group which are best carried out by smaller groups, either within or outside the class session. This is true where the class or society is fairly large and where the experienced teacher or leader has available several helpers. If the size of the room permits, these committees may withdraw to different corners for their planning. Sometimes there are other corners in the church where such committees may meet if the group is well enough under control so that the teacher can be sure that they will proceed with their work in businesslike fashion. An assistant may accompany these groups, but he should be careful not to dictate and dominate the planning. In some cases, where the class sits around a table, a committee may meet around each end of the table to plan. Then these two committees may meet toward the close of the class session and report to the rest of the group the result of their committee work. In other cases these committees may volunteer to meet at some time outside the class and to report on the following Sunday.

An Activity Period

Sometimes in the midst of a project there comes the necessity for a work period within the Church School hour. How to make this period profitable and not distracting to other class groups sometimes taxes the ingenuity of teachers, especially when the equipment and facilities are not adjusted to this type of class session. Miss R and her class group were studying a unit on Paul's life and journeys. Members of the class wished to make maps showing Paul's journeys that could be used in the department. The only time they could make these was during the Sunday morning session, since many members of the group lived at long distances from the church and could not come back during the week. The teacher puzzled over the matter. " How can we study the lesson and still get the maps made? And how can I direct the conversation to the subject at hand so that it will not be merely desultory, aimless conversation? " she wondered. The class procured the needed materials and, with maps and Bibles, began to list the places to which Paul went. Two in the group worked on sketching the outline of the Mediterranean Sea and of the countries surrounding it, with the guidance of another map. Two set to work to find out about the places mentioned in the Bible where Paul stopped. They listed these on the board. Two others looked up in a Bible dictionary all that they could find about these places today. One was reading at the browsing table from Morton's " In the Steps of St. Paul," [1] describing his visit to each place. As they found interesting items they put them down in their

[1] Morton, H. V., " In the Steps of St. Paul." Dodd, Mead & Company, 1936.

notebooks and told the others about them. The teacher or members of the group would read alternately about Paul's visit to these places in the first century and the traveler's twentieth century visit to these places or their ruins. Questions came up in the midst of this procedure as to the mechanics of map-drawing. The group discussed these as well as the questions which bore more directly on the Pauline journeys.

In a certain Weekday Church School a group was busy at work putting together mimeographed copies of songs to make a little hymnbook. Each one had his own share of the process to carry through. Some were pasting, some were tying, some were arranging pages, and still others were pasting colored pictures on the cover of each book. There was a selection of pictures from which to choose. Informally the teacher raised the question, when they were using the picture of Christ and the Doctors, by Hofmann, " If you had a person who you were sure could give you exactly the right answer to some question about God or religion, what question would you ask? " The boy across the table from the leader, the chief troublemaker in class and the despair of his public-school teacher, leaned across and asked wistfully, " What does life mean anyway? " With that as a start several gave their ideas, still working busily with their hands. Then the question came back to the one who asked it, who said: " Oh, it means to grow up, get married, have a family. You know." With not a smile from the others, the discussion turned to the importance of each person as a link in the chain which binds past and future together. The group began to think back into the beginnings of things and to look forward into the future like men, and not at all like the gang of troublemaking lads who had started out together in this Weekday Church School club. But it is doubtful if any such question would have been asked had it not been that hands were busy and the group had been welded into a congenial fellowship.

An Appreciation Session

Miss F was a young college student who was teaching a group of highly sophisticated junior high school girls in a suburban community church. She was in the midst of a unit, the aim of which was to give perspective to the entire Bible story from Genesis to Revelation. She had come to the place in the unit where the subject for the lesson was to be the life, work, and death of Jesus. She selected for her procedure that morning the question-and-answer method. The real aim of this lesson was to help the group to love Jesus and respond appreciatively to the beauty of his life story. But the method she used was an analytical one, suited to the analysis and discussion of everyday problems and not designed to lead to the development of attitudes of appreciation. Consequently the hour was spent in discussion back and forth. Even the events leading up to the crucifixion were treated in this same manner and, it seemed to the observer, the girls left the class with little conception of the power and the beauty of this story of the life of Christ.

In this situation, one of several methods would probably have been more successful. First, the story of Jesus' life might have been told from birth to resurrection. This would need to be done effectively. Or copies of some of the world's great paintings of scenes from the life of Christ might have been shown and interpreted in an appreciative way.[2] Or beautiful poems which interpret different aspects or events in his life might have been used. Or the members of the class might have imagined that they were looking at scenes from Jesus' life thrown on a screen and different girls might have described these vividly enough so that the others could see them in their imagination.

Perhaps, as a result of this class experience, some individual in the group could have been encouraged or inspired to do some creative writing of his own, either in story or poetical form.

A clear distinction, then, should be made between the class session that has for its aim the stimulating of wholesome emotional attitudes and the session that aims to sharpen the discrimination of pupils through careful analysis of problematic issues.

The following suggestions [3] for a session intended to develop emotional patterns may be helpful:

1. Adequate preparation should precede the stimulation of emotional response. Pupils should be atuned to the situation.

2. The materials should be within the understanding of the pupils.

3. No attempt should be made to develop an emotional reaction to the same degree of intensity in all pupils.

4. Informal procedures are more effective than formal procedures.

5. The teacher, by his own actions, must give true evidence that he possesses the pattern being developed in the pupils.

6. Analytic treatment, as a general rule, should be deferred until the pupil acquires sufficient interest to request it.

[2] "Christ and the Fine Arts," by Cynthia P. Maus, would be useful here. Harper & Brothers, 1938.

[3] Umstattd, J. G., "Secondary School Teaching," pages 279 ff. Ginn and Company, 1937. Used by permission.

7. The emotional pattern should be permitted to develop gradually.

8. Frequent opportunity should be given for the use of the response.

Use of Resource Persons

Very often a group feels the need of expert advice or of information not easily available in books. The teacher may not be versed in the matter and should feel free to confess his lack of knowledge. But there may be someone in the church or the community who has firsthand information which he is willing to share with a group. Such a person should be informed as to what the group is attempting to do and what aspects of the question are of particular interest. Members of the group may interview this person and explain their wishes to him. Then this resource person may speak through the class hour on points concerning which the group wishes information. Time should be left, however, for members of the group to ask questions. Sometimes the entire class hour may be given over to the asking of questions on the part of the group and the answering of them by this special resource leader. One group in Weekday Church School spent a very fascinating series of sessions learning about different countries and their customs, and Christian missions in these lands, from missionaries and missionary children who dressed in native costume, brought along objects of various sorts, gave very brief talks, and then let the boys and girls ask whatever questions came to them. The following session was spent in discussing in class what had been learned from the previous session and in planning for the next outside resource leader.

A Period for Written Work or Creative Expression

According to an old-time method, the leader would write on the blackboard or tell the members of his group what they were to write down in their notebooks. Each notebook looked very much like every other, with but little opportunity for creativity. The work was judged by its similarity to the model, not by its divergence from it. With the new pupils' work books used in some closely graded courses written work combined with discussion becomes a very important procedure throughout the class session. The teacher should put a premium upon originality and attempts at artistic ways of expressing thoughts and feelings. If a leader wishes to know what some junior high school pupils can do, artistically and creatively, he is advised to turn through the pages of Creative Expression, edited and published by the Progressive Education Association.

One eighth-grade boy greatly enjoyed making pictures of Bible scenes. They were unusually artistic for a boy of his age. One thirteen-year-old girl in an art class chose for the subject of her picture City Feet. It showed only the feet of people along a city pavement. In a class project of making a book of religion, the group was organized as an editorial staff. It was interesting that, although no special emphasis had been laid upon it, occasionally a class member would contribute a poem to go into this " book of religion."

One creative teacher asked the members of a group to paint pictures showing imaginary scenes from the boyhood of Jesus in Nazareth. These pictures gave him a great deal of insight into their ideas of Palestinian life and their conception of Jesus.

Bible Study

It is the deep-seated conviction of most Christian teachers in the Church School that boys and girls should come to know the Bible, to appreciate it, and to use it as a guide for their daily living. But many will agree that at this point the Church School is failing in its task. The average boy and girl are now growing into manhood and womanhood with an appalling lack of Biblical knowledge, and also with little appreciation of its value and its usefulness in daily living.

Throughout the class sessions of the Church School the Bible should be used purposefully as a familiar and much appreciated source book. Copies should be available in the King James (or Authorized) and the American Standard Versions. These copies should be in good condition. They should also be printed in fairly large type so that boys and girls will not find reading difficult. Many teachers find it helpful to use some of the modern translations occasionally, to throw new light on the meaning of certain passages and to help the group to see how up-to-date the Bible really is. Other tools for the study of the Bible should be available, such as a good Bible dictionary, a Bible atlas or some good Bible maps, and a good concordance. Boys and girls should be taught how to use these.

To many boys and girls, and also to some adults, the Bible is made up of a jumble of characters, incidents, teachings, and admonitions, without any clear continuity or sequence in the Biblical story. One very intelligent " quartet " of junior high school boys, when asked to place one Old Testament character in each of the five-hundred-year periods preceding the birth of

Christ, found that they were unable to do so. They had little idea as to whether Moses, David, Abraham, or Nehemiah came first in the Bible story. A very simple device for gaining perspective is the use of a time line or a time chart, on which equal spaces are marked off for the different centuries and events are placed in their proper chronological relationship to each other. Sometimes these time charts may be enlarged and illustrated, forming murals for departmental rooms. They are, of course, built up gradually from week to week and from month to month, the pupils themselves placing on the charts in the correct positions the various characters and incidents which they are studying.

Sometimes groups are interested in discovering the various literary forms in the Bible. It is fascinating to learn that Biblical poetry has a structure all its own. For this sort of approach to Bible study an American Standard rather than a King James Version should be used, since the latter does not show the difference between prose and poetry.

But, most frequently, there is need for a more intensive study of a particular incident, or passage, to discover its meaning for us today. The secret of making this kind of Bible study interesting and fruitful is the attempt to recapture the vividness of the experience which lies back of the words and then to lay it down beside the experience which boys and girls are having here and now, to discover points of similarity between the two. To recapture the experience from the past, one needs to get down beneath the words, quaint as they sometimes may seem; beneath the differing customs and ways of thinking, in such contrast to

twentieth century customs in our Western civilization
— down to the real folks who lived in the past and had
these experiences. For this, an understanding of Hebrew and first-century Christian customs and ways of
thought is necessary. One also needs a vivid imagination to live with these people of the past and to make
their experiences one's own. A story from the Bible
must first live in the mind and the imagination of the
teacher before the teacher can succeed in making it
live in the mind of the pupil. If the Bible is to become
a vital and a living book to this generation of younger
adolescents, its experiences must be linked in a very
real and vital way with the experiences which boys
and girls are having here and now in the twentieth
century.

It is evident that no timeworn device of reading
around the class a Bible passage or story, stopping at
each verse to comment or to raise questions, will accomplish the ends we desire. Often a silent reading of
the story or passage will be more effective. But this
silent reading should be preceded by building up in the
mind and the imagination of the pupils a background
and an understanding of the experience to be studied,
as well as calling to their minds certain similar experiences of their own. Let us see to it that the reading of
various passages or parts of the Bible becomes a purposeful undertaking. Let us avoid the taking up of
the Bible to read a passage in class just because it
happens to be the lesson for a particular Sunday or
because references to the passage appear at the beginning of the lesson treatment. The Bible will become
more vital to boys and girls if they see in it that which
will meet *their* various needs, guide *them* in living a

good life, throw light on the various problems *they* are facing, and express in a beautiful and inspiring way experiences which *they* themselves are having.

Often the working out of a story in dramatic form will help to make it vivid and real to the group. Sometimes a study of different interpretations of the same Biblical incident by various artists will be helpful. Sometimes, the making of dioramas or miniature stages depicting certain Old Testament stories will challenge careful and thorough study.

In studying some of the proverbs, one group of girls in a Weekday Church School class imagined the wisemen sitting in the gates of a Jewish city observing the community life as it went on around them. Certain members of the class then undertook to pantomime the various types of persons whom the wisemen observed, as described in The Proverbs. The others attempted to guess which proverbs they were pantomiming. This, of course, meant a rather intensive study of the various types of people described in this book of the Bible, such as lazy folks, nagging women, drunken sots, bargainers, and king's messengers. The members of the group were surprised to discover how modern and up-to-date the book of The Proverbs really is. To carry this project still farther, a group might decide to observe people on the street or in the community and then undertake to write some modern proverbs after the style of the Hebrew wisemen.

Excursions or Pilgrimages

These are probably not so easily managed in connection with the Sunday Church School session as in connection with an Intermediate missionary society or a

Weekday or Vacation Church School. Here is an account of what one society group did [4]:

" The young people of the Junior High School Society of Faith Church, Springfield (Congregational), decided to visit some institutions, and it occurred to them that on these visits they might be able to make some contributions that would be appreciated. One of their number played a Hawaiian guitar, another the piano, one could sing, one could give dramatic readings, and so forth. It was not difficult to work out a Sunday afternoon program in lieu of their regular 5.45 P.M. meeting. At one Sunday evening meeting they would make plans for the next week's visitation, considering what they would do and at what points they ought to be careful. On the Sunday following the visitation they always had as a theme for discussion: ' What about this institution? Was there anything wrong in our social order which made it necessary? What could they do toward better class or race relationships? '

" They made eight or nine visitations. When they went to the hospital just before Christmas they took with them presents tagged: ' For a boy — years old'; ' For a girl . . .' They went to the Old Men's Home, having discovered that it had few visitors, whereas most of the attention was concentrated on the Old Ladies' Home. Their schedule included the County Home and Orphan Asylum and a School for the Blind; and everywhere they gave their program. One of their best visits was to the group of ninety young people of St. John's Congregational Church (colored), a delightful interracial occasion."

Pilgrimages or excursions may be the prelude to worth-while discussions or projects of various kinds. In a certain denominational paper plans for society topics for one month were built around the idea of pilgrimages.

[4] Reported from Missionary Education Bulletin, World Fellowship. Division of Christian Education, Congregational and Christian Churches, Winter, 1934–1935. Used by permission.

These pilgrimages, called "Trails to Hallowed Places," were as follows:

"A Soldier's Grave (Peace)."
"The Town Hall (Making Our City Christian)."
"An Ancestral Home (New Christian Ways of Getting Along in Families)."
"The Church Cornerstone (Church History)." [5]

Whenever this type of procedure is used, the trips should be carefully planned beforehand. Members of the expedition should know what they are to look for so that they will be intelligent observers. All the mechanical details such as transportation (if necessary), street-crossing, et cetera, should be arranged beforehand and directions clearly given. When visiting a church or some other institution, the head of the institution should be informed of your visit and an appointment made. Following the visit there should be a summing up of observations or evaluations.

Planning a Worship Service

In some departments when each class takes its turn in being responsible for the worship service, a session may occasionally be devoted to the planning of the worship service for a given Sunday. Or a committee from the Intermediate Christian Endeavor may meet with the adult counselor for this purpose. If this service of worship is to emphasize some phase of a unit being studied in the classes or the topic to be discussed, the planning affords a special chance to talk over together the values from this unit which are real to the

[5] See "Program Builder," November, 1938, pages 14, 21. Presbyterian Church, U. S., Richmond, Virginia. Used by permission.

individuals in the group. A theme should be chosen and talked over together from its various angles. Then the hymns and the Scripture should be chosen which will most effectively develop the theme. Sometimes a picture interpretation may become the center of this brief service, or a story, or a beautiful poem. Perhaps a special worship setting for the service may be planned. Time limits should be considered and strictly adhered to. Responsibilities for the various parts of the service should be distributed. All the details should be worked out so that the service will proceed smoothly and each part be integrated into the other parts. Above all, help your committee to see the importance of this task of leading a group of people into an experience of worship. Avoid letting it become mechanical or trivial.

A Summing Up or Evaluation Period

Whatever the unit or enterprise, at the conclusion of it there should be a period of evaluation when the work is viewed critically and plans for future improvement made. If a good bit of new information has been gained it is often a satisfying experience for the group to take a simple objective test of some sort which will measure, in one way at least, the result of effort.

A Culmination

Most units or courses should have some sort of culminating feature at the end to which the group can look forward, and toward which the members can work. This may be something within the class or within the department or within the club. It may be the packing of a box or an exhibit to which parents or other classes in the department are invited. It may be a play or a social affair with a program as one feature. It may take many forms, but it adds the element of purposefulness to work and study.

The Expanded Session

" But," perhaps some bewildered leader will ask, " how can we ever expect to do these things in the brief twenty-five or thirty minutes allowed us in our class periods on Sunday morning? "

It is true that some of the procedures described in this chapter require longer sessions than are possible in the regular Sunday School hour. Because of this fact some Church Schools are turning to expanded sessions as the partial solution of their problem. Sometimes plans are made for the members of a group to meet for two hours on Sunday morning. Sometimes they meet on a Sunday afternoon or on some evening during the week. In this expanded session more of the informal procedures may be used, such as dramatization, the carrying out of service projects, visits to interesting places, and creative expression in its various forms. Where this is the arrangement, the first regular Church School hour may be given over to group planning and to the study and investigation and discussion which will be basic in carrying out the project. But there will be an essential element added to a class session which is to be followed later by a period for work. The members of the group will have an added motivation. They know that they are to do something about it, that their study is for a definite social purpose — to carry forward an important enterprise to which they have committed themselves.

Many other methods, such as storytelling and memorization, will not be treated in this chapter. They are familiar enough so that leaders can handle them more easily when the occasion calls for them. With the addition of the newer procedures, the teacher will have a greater variety from which to choose, which, it is hoped, will result in greater educational effectiveness in class and club group.

Suggestions for Further Reading and Study

Blair, W. Dyer, " The New Vacation Church School," Chapters 4–8. Harper & Brothers, 1934.

Carrier, Blanche, " How Shall I Learn to Teach Religion? " Harper & Brothers, 1931.

Elliott, H. S., " Group Discussion in Religious Education." Association Press, 1930.

Maus, Cynthia P., " Christ and the Fine Arts." See especially the introduction for suggestions on the use of pictures, poetry, and hymn interpretations. Harper & Brothers, 1938.

Smith, Robert Seneca, " New Trails for the Christian Teacher." The Westminster Press, 1934.

" Methods of Church Work with Intermediates," pages 8–12. Methodist Board of Education, 740 Rush Street, Chicago, Illinois.

CHAPTER VII

PREPARING YOUNGER ADOLESCENTS FOR VITAL CHURCH MEMBERSHIP

PERHAPS you are saying to yourself, " It is all very well to talk about various methods and materials, but if boys and girls fail to become vital Christians and members of the Christian Church, the program fails at its most crucial point."

This is indeed true. Unless these two important goals are realized no program of Christian education has been successful. It is time to face this question squarely and honestly. Is your local church recruiting and preparing younger adolescent boys and girls for their place in the Christian fellowship of the Church? Or is it letting them slip away from its influence at this crucial time, thinking, perhaps, that it may win them back to itself when they have grown older and more mature?

What methods for winning the loyalty of Intermediates to the Church and the cause it represents and for training them to share in its enterprises does your local church use? Consult your pastor. Find out what methods he believes should be used. What courses in your Church School curriculum emphasize this important objective? In what other phases of the entire Intermediate program is this emphasis also given?

What Vital Church Membership Means

Different communions vary in their beliefs concerning the religious status of children before they are old enough to " join the Church " or to be confirmed. Some consider them " outside the fold " until they have made their own decision, confessed Christ, and become Christians. In other church communions all children are " within the fold " because they have been born into the families of church members within the parish. They are brought up within the Church and do not know what it means to be considered " outsiders " so far as their relationship to the Church is concerned.

But all church communions will agree that it is desirable and important that these growing boys and girls become *vital* church members, and not mere *nominal* members who take their church vows lightly. By vital church membership is meant a growing loyalty to the Church and its enterprises, local and world-wide; a willingness to share its responsibilities; and an ability and willingness to gain spiritual help from its services of worship and its means of grace.

Youth Needs the Christian Church

Boys and girls of Intermediate age need the Christian Church. They need its Christian fellowship, its services of worship, its opportunities for co-operative Kingdom service. In order to attain to the highest type of Christian personality development they need a sense of belonging to such a divine institution. There will probably not be another period in their lives when the need for belonging to something worth while is so keenly felt. They will outgrow the programs of many other organizations, such as the Boy Scouts and the Girl Scouts, but the Church should have an increasing claim on their loyalty as they grow older and more mature.

The Church Needs Youth

On the other hand, the Christian Church needs these boys and girls. They bring to it marvelous potentialities and powers, which, if wisely enlisted, directed, and developed, should mean much for the future of the Church as it faces its work in the world. These boys and girls are the Church's greatest human assets. If these potential assets are neglected, the Church cannot hope to survive. It is a sobering thought that Christ still depends on human instruments to carry on his work in the world. Without such instruments the Church will not have hands and feet to carry on its program. And the chief source of recruits for the Christian Church today is from the Church School.

Winning and Training Them for the Church

One of the most important tasks, therefore, for pastor and for church leaders is this one of recruiting for Christ and the Church these younger adolescents and then training them for their new responsibilities. While many pastors and church leaders realize the importance of this work, some of them are sincerely puzzled as to the most effective methods to be employed.

Some churches and pastors have depended on securing decisions for Christ through emotional appeals, in revival services, in special Church School Decision Days, or in the privacy of the class group. Boys and girls, on these special occasions, have been urged to " take a stand for Christ." In some cases the appeal is successful. Many an earnest Christian teacher or pastor looks back to the day when someone within the Church led him to make a decision for Christ.

In other situations, the pastor and the church leaders depend upon the Church School teacher to exert influence at the proper psychological time when boys and girls are especially responsive to religious influence, and thus to lead them to accept Christ. In many cases there is excellent co-operation between teachers, parents, and pastors in this evangelistic undertaking.

The home, of course, must share in this, for it furnishes the background experiences, the appreciations, and the Christian examples which are often the most important factors in the decision to lead a Christian life. A call in the home by the pastor or the Church School teacher and a talk with the parent may lead to a decision from a growing boy or girl, if there is a happy relationship existing between the boy or girl and these adult counselors.

In some cases when there is a particularly congenial relationship between pastor and Intermediates, or between Intermediates and their Church School teachers, personal conversations initiated by the boys or girls themselves may lead to the expression of a desire for church membership. This method of personal counseling may be considered one of the most effective methods for recruiting church members.

The Confirmation Class

In some churches it is considered quite the normal thing for boys and girls of church parents to enter a confirmation class at a certain age and be prepared for confirmation and entrance into the Christian Church. In most Lutheran communities and in many other communions this practice of having a confirmation class prevails. The class is usually taught by the pastor or by his assistant for a period of from eight to ten weeks in the interval between Christmas and Palm Sunday or Easter. Some of these classes meet on Sunday morning at the Church School hour, some meet on Saturday morning, and still others meet after school on some afternoon during the week. Standards for attendance and work are apt to be somewhat higher than in the Church School class. In some cases boys and girls are even excused from public school to attend these classes. This fact increases their importance in the eyes of the pupils. Parents also feel that this instruction is especially important, so they see to it that their children attend regularly.

There is great variation when it comes to the question of the content of this instruction. Many pastors depend upon the use of the catechism. This is studied, explained, and memorized. Other pastors emphasize instruction in the Bible also. Still others include some study of church history and of church organization. A study of the different features of a church worship service is included by some. Explanation of the sacraments of baptism and the Lord's Supper is usually given. In many classes boys and girls are told about the financial responsibilities of church members. Some enterprising pastors take their young people into the church sanctuary and explain to them the meaning of the various church symbols and parts of the church edifice. Still others feel the need of helping boys and girls to build an adequate philosophy of life of their own, so they encourage them to ask religious and ethical questions in which they feel the need of help.

Listed at the end of this chapter are a number of courses in training for church membership which have been used successfully by some pastors and leaders.

Within the Church School Department

Another method of preparing boys and girls for intelligent church membership is the use of the regular channels of the Church School curriculum and program in the Sunday School, denominational Weekday Church School, and Vacation Church School. Most of the Closely Graded and the Group or Departmental Graded lesson courses today include units centering in the Christian Church, its history, its program, and its responsibilities. The Church School teacher then cooperates with the pastor in this process of training for church membership. The Christian Nurture Course developed and used by the Protestant Episcopal Church is noteworthy for its emphasis upon churchmanship throughout the Church School curriculum. Some of these graded courses prepared by the denominations suggest projects Intermediate boys and girls may carry through, which, if the pastor avails himself of the opportunity, will bring them into closer relationship with him.

The Junior Church

Another method of developing ability to participate in the church program which has been experimented with considerably during the last ten years is the junior church or some adaptation of this plan. In some cases this junior or youth congregation meets in a separate service on Sunday morning. A formal service is conducted with boys and girls assisting as ushers, members of the choir, and so forth. Occasionally this junior congregation is organized according to the denominational pattern, with junior session or vestrymen or official board, as the case may be. This plan aims to give younger members of a church constituency experience in conducting a church organization.

In one large, wealthy suburban church the pastor, with his four or five student pastor assistants alternating, conducts a service for the younger congregation at 9.30 A.M. in the church auditorium, with a junior choir assisting. This service takes the place of a regular departmental service of worship for Senior, Intermediate, and Junior Departments. They adjourn from this service to attend their regular class sessions in the educational building.

In some churches members of the junior congregation assemble for the adult service, sitting in the front of the sanctuary, and then, after the opening of the service and a brief junior sermon or story, are dismissed to an extended period in which activities more suited to their age level are carried on. Some of these plans for a junior congregation are of doubtful value for older Intermediate boys and girls, who, if prepared for it, should begin to get real meaning and value from the regular service of the church.

Perhaps a more practicable working plan is the one in which, during the last year of the Junior Department or the first year of the Intermediate Department, a very definite effort is made to interpret the church service of worship to the members of a group and to help them to understand its value and its meaning. For example, in one church, they make a point of going into the church service in a body on Sunday and then discussing all parts of this service, the meaning and the significance of each. As a part of this careful training for adult worship, the members of the group entering the full church relationship are prepared to take Communion together on a certain Sunday before they share in the adult Communion service in the church.

One of the most useful factors in this preparation for church membership is to make sure that throughout all their experience in connection with the church and its various organizations none of these are thought of or spoken of as separate and distinct institutions demanding separate and distinct loyalties, but are thought of as the Church itself, functioning in different ways and with different groups. If this impression of a single institution demanding undivided loyalty has been created, boys and girls will then feel that they are already a vital part of the Church before they take the step which brings them into full communion.

Enrollment in the Church School should be considered an automatic enrollment in the ongoing program of the church. Those enrolled in this way should be led to feel that their attendance and participation in the program are vitally important to the whole church as well as to the Church School. Throughout the years when they are growing up they are gradually given insights into what church fellowship means. The worship services in the various departments, if carefully planned and reverently carried through, give valuable training in participation in worship which will help them later to enter into the adult service of worship. Perhaps at different times and on different occasions the age group may make some contribution to the adult service of worship in an effective way. The members of the group will also be learning about the program of the church and having experience in sharing in this program as they are able. Thus, the whole idea of attending the morning service of worship and having a part in the church program as a full member becomes a climax in their experience to look forward to with anticipation. When they enter the junior high school department of the Church School they may be given the opportunity to decide for themselves whether they will unite with the church in full membership. To be sure, they have never been allowed to consider themselves outsiders, but this decision for themselves gives dignity and new meaning to the next step they are about to take. The special instruction following their decision to unite with the Church in full membership will not be something isolated or tacked on. It will be a summarizing, a re-emphasizing, and a supplementing of the things that they have been learning throughout the entire Church School program.

Understanding the Church Background

The pastor or leader who wishes to bring boys and girls into a vital relationship to the church fellowship should know thoroughly the church background of each of these whom he is seeking to guide. There is such a crisscross of church relationship and affiliation in the average American family today that this may not be so simple as it seems, even in so-called church families. A combined Protestant and Roman Catholic background is likely to cause great difficulties in the thinking of a boy or a girl, even though it is very clear that the child is to be brought up in the Protestant faith. Then there is the question whether a boy or a girl comes from an ultraconservative fundamentalist or a liberal background. Children coming from conservative religious backgrounds are not apt to respond readily to liberal teachings and the parents will be even less enthusiastic about it. On the other hand, many liberal-minded parents and their children may not respond readily to certain conservative theological and Biblical points of view which the parents have long ago discarded. There is also the difference between the extremely liturgical church, the church of emotional revivalistic temperament, and the church of extreme simplicity, such as one belonging to the Society of Friends.

Any group of boys and girls will have within it those who have varying concepts and ideas of religion and of the church. These ideas may come from their homes or from their friends or from previous experiences in church or Church School. Boys and girls may seem antagonistic toward the church because their parents have been overstrict in the matter of church attendance and behavior. Or they may feel that the church is of little importance because their parents give little time and attention to it. At least they are very apt to reflect the attitudes of their parents or the opposite. Some boys and girls may be bored with the service because the pastor has not made this service appealing to them.

One of the preliminary things, then, which should be done in any class training for church membership is to get at the real thinking of the members of the group as soon as possible. Certain printed tests are helpful at this point.

Such tests are:

"Ways of the Church." A series of tests developed by the National Council, Department of Religious Education, Protestant Episcopal Church, Church Mission House, 281 Fourth Avenue, New York, N. Y.

"The Church and Church Membership." International Council of Religious Education. (Also found on pages 195 ff. in Lucile Desjardins, "Our Living Church.")

Culminating Features

The training class for church membership should lead up to the experience of the Communion service. However, in some churches candidates are required to meet the session, or official body of the church, or some representatives from it, and answer questions, thus giving evidence of their eligibility for church membership. This may prove a very difficult and embarrassing experience for some reticent boys and girls. On the other hand it may be an experience which anticipates a helpful fellowship between those who are older and more mature and the less experienced prospective church member.

The following suggestions are given in one textbook on training for church membership [1]:

Put the candidate at ease.

Eliminate a sense of hurry and confusion.

Give the candidate a lasting and inspiring impression of the examination.

Discover the real motives, purpose, spiritual development, and possibilities of the candidate.

Discover the spiritual need of the candidate and report to the church leaders.

[1] Knight, W. D., "Preparing Young People for Church Membership," page 7. The Westminster Press, 1938.

Leave with the candidate an increased respect and love for the Church of Christ and a desire to be of genuine service to it.

Leave with the candidate the feeling that joining the Church is not an end, but a vital step in a continuing and developing Christian life.

The First Communion Service

The first Communion service should be a memorable occasion in the life of the boy or girl participating. Careful preparation and explanation should, of course, be given as to how to make the most fruitful use of the silent moments for prayer and meditation, after the cup and the bread have been served.

The public entrance into the Church and the public confession of faith should by no means be a casual or a hurried affair. There should be an individual touch to it. " The laying on of the hands " has a very real spiritual as well as psychological value. The true minister will have a personal touch for each boy or girl. The members of the group should, of course, in the training class have been taught the questions which are to be put to them by the officiating clergyman, and the proper answers, so that they will be saved any moments of delay and consequent embarrassment.

Some churches plan reunions for their new members. Sometimes these are connected with annual pre-Communion services for young people or Communion anniversaries.

Whatever is planned, the church should guard against giving any idea to boys and girls that, with their first Communion and entrance into full membership, they have graduated from the educational program of the church, and no longer need to attend Church School. This is one of the tragic misconceptions which too frequently accompanies the practice of confirmation classes.

Service in the Church

A church should not think of its boys and girls as established unless they have found a real opportunity for service. It is important for the official body of the church and its leaders to find satisfactory tasks and responsibilities in the ongoing church program which these younger members may undertake and which will be worthy of their wholehearted effort. Too often when boys and girls come eagerly to leaders saying: " Now that I belong, what can I do to help? " these same leaders look puzzled and suggest: " You can come to church and Sunday School every Sunday. You can study your lessons. You can be good. And, perhaps, you can bring your friends if they don't belong to some other church." When these same boys and girls ask further, " What else? " there seems to be nothing else to say, and they go away feeling somewhat " let down." In every other club to which they belong, membership means responsibility and active duties to perform.

Junior high school pupils are really capable of doing worth-while things if they have good leadership. Here are some of the things boys and girls of this age have done in some churches:

Sung in a junior choir.
Acted as ushers on special occasions or in the evening.
Run the mimeograph and helped to prepare the church bulletin.
Planned and participated in special worship services or dramatic presentations.
Addressed envelopes for a busy pastor or secretary.
Distributed dodgers or circulars from house to house.

Chapter VIII

LEADERS ARE NEEDED

As a pastor or a departmental superintendent, have you ever felt discouraged because you find it so difficult to secure and keep efficient leaders for your Intermediate classes or society groups?

Or perhaps you are one of those persons whom the pastor or superintendent has asked to teach an Intermediate group. You are hesitating, at the same time asking yourself such pointed questions as: " What have I to share with these boys and girls? " and " What do I need to learn in order to be an effective leader? "

Or you may be a leader who feels utterly discouraged because you consider that you are not measuring up to the responsibility which was thrust upon you before you were ready for it. You are thinking of giving up your class. You feel sure that there are others much more capable than you who would be willing to take it.

But pause a moment and consider anew the decision which you are making. Remember that a sense of inadequacy is God's way of telling us that we should look to him for strength and guidance for the task he has entrusted to us. Face honestly and squarely any light that may come to you in this chapter with regard to your own personal characteristics and your personal opportunities for further preparation for the teaching task. Try the following:

Make a list of qualities that you think a leader of Intermediate boys or girls should possess. After each

item in this list place a mark for yourself, grading
yourself either *good, fair,* or *poor,* for this quality. If
you do not trust your own judgment, ask some friend
whose judgment you trust, to grade you in each of
these qualities. Now compare this list that you have
made with the list of qualities given in this chapter to
see how they differ. Take the one personal characteristic in which you have graded yourself lowest. Begin,
with God's help, to make a change in your life at this
point. This challenging attempt should bring to you a
new sense of spiritual vitality.

On pages 140–142 of this chapter you will find a list of
the various activities sometimes carried on by leaders.
Study this list very thoughtfully. If there is any item
here which you do not consider the function of a leader
of Intermediates, place a question mark in front of it.
Check each of these activities which you, at some time
or other, carry on with your Intermediates. Are there
any of these which you feel you are neglecting? If so,
which ones? In which of these do you feel the need of
help most acutely? Plan some way of getting some
assistance at this point in your leadership.

Now make a list of the ways in which your departmental superintendent or someone in your church or
community has helped you to improve the quality of
your leadership. What have you done on your own
account to improve your effectiveness as a leader?
What have you done to help others to improve the effectiveness of their leadership?

The Kind of Leaders Needed

" I should rather teach younger children, or even the
older folks — but please don't give me Intermediates."

This is the plea occasionally heard in Church Schools. Very often Intermediate boys and girls are left teacherless. They drift into the practice of loafing through a class period, or attempt to teach their own class at the suggestion of a desperate superintendent, or find themselves put temporarily into a class of older young people, where they feel they do not belong, or they gradually drift away from Church School attendance.

And yet this is one age particularly in need of skilled and adequate leadership. For the leader who has the Christian personality and experience, the patience, and the insight, there comes a strategic opportunity to influence growing life in a permanent way. But not every person can measure up to the standard set by these young people themselves.

A group of junior high school pupils in a private school gave the following description of what they considered the makings of a *good teacher*. The ingredients were as follows [1]:

A good teacher —
Gives only helpful criticism and encourages better work.
Joins with class activities.
Understands the pupil's side.
Does not expect the same of everybody.
Is not too easy, but keeps you encouraged.
Is patient.
Distributes home work evenly.
Has a real interest in the subject he teaches, but also knows about things generally as well as his own subject.
Doesn't fuss.

[1] Carpenter, Louise, " Keeping Awake in Your Mind," pages 254–259. Progressive Education Magazine, April, 1936. Used by permission.

Can make people see what he is talking about, so that they can understand and learn his subject with interest.

Is on time for classes.

Can recognize a joke and take one.

Helps when you don't understand work.

In an investigation of the traits of successful junior high school teachers, the following ranked highest [2]:

1. Attractiveness.
2. Considerateness.
3. Co-operation.
4. Enthusiasm.
5. Forcefulness.
6. Good judgment.
7. Industry.
8. Magnetism.
9. Neatness.
10. Promptness.

It is interesting to note in the list made by boys and girls themselves what an important place such qualities as understanding, consideration, patience, and insight had in their thinking.

Patterns for Living

The younger adolescent is seeking a pattern according to which he may build his own life. He needs to see that pattern embodied in living form. For the adolescent girl the leader should be one, if possible, who embodies the social charm and grace which the girl hopes to see realized in her own life someday. This does not necessarily mean that the leader should have a beauti-

[2] Waples, Douglas, and Charters, W. W., " Commonwealth Teacher-Training Study." University of Chicago Press, 1929. Used by permission.

ful face and dress expensively. Some very plain people, plainly dressed and with plain features, have an inner beauty that reflects itself in face and actions. At no time in life is the adage more true, " What you are . . . thunders so that I cannot hear what you say." Through a wholesome, attractive Christian personality, a leader may guide early adolescent youth straight to the feet of Christ, the supremely attractive Personality.

In the " Pilot's Guide-book " [3] the following qualifications for Pioneer leaders are given. They come closer than the list on page 138 to picturing the ideal Christian leader of junior high school youth.

1. A sense of the spirit of adventure in everyday living.
2. An understanding comradeship with boys and girls.
3. An insight into their natural interests and talents.
4. A confidence in their initiative and ability.
5. A determination to be helpful without dominating the situation.
6. An eagerness to enlist every member in Pioneer activity.
7. An appreciation of individual effort and teamwork.
8. A conviction regarding the need of Jesus Christ in everyday life.
9. An attitude of faith, resulting in a willingness, after having done one's best, to leave the final outcome with God.

One successful leader of adolescent girls says:

" Who, then, is equipped to be a leader of girls? Clearly, it is the person who herself believes in life and its potentialities; who is facing her own problems with honesty, integrity, and serenity; who has faith in the life and the potentialities of the adolescent girl; who demands that she shall have a chance to find love and achievement in an ever-widening circle of ac-

[3] The Pioneer Plan, " Pilot's Guide-book," page 19. The Judson Press. Used by permission.

tivities and relationships; and who can help her to an ever-deepening and enriching participation in the life of all mankind and of the universe." [4]

May not this same hold true also for the leader of adolescent boys?

The Responsibility of Guidance

But perhaps the prospective leader will say: " Yes, I realize that it is important to act sincerely as a Christian and to have an attractive Christian personality and a real Christian experience; but there must be still more to this business of teaching. What shall I be expected to do as a teacher? "

Let us analyze some of the things that a skillful leader will need to do at times, if he is to make full use of his opportunities to guide growing life toward the realization of the goals of Christian education.[5]

1. The leader of youth will need, at times, to discover or locate the interests and needs of his group, or of individuals within his group.

2. He will need to be on the lookout for projects or enterprises which will express these interests in a tangible way and will meet these needs.

3. He will need to know how to initiate projects or to guide the group in a wise choice of projects best suited to their own interests and needs without seeming to impose something on them.

[4] Elliott, Grace L., " Understanding the Adolescent Girl," pages 133, 134. Henry Holt and Company, Inc., 1930. Used by permission.

[5] Compare the list of functions of a leader given in " Growth in Christian Service: Suggested Pathways to More Effective Service in the Christian Cause." International Council of Religious Education, 1937.

4. He will need to help the members of his group to develop an adequate motivation in connection with a chosen enterprise which will raise the level of their purposing and bind them into a closer unity.

5. He will need to know how to make every member of the group feel that he really belongs, that he has status in the group; and he will need to build up the solidarity of the group relationships, at the same time working toward a broadening of their outlook and interests.

6. He will need to know where he can lay his hands upon enriching and interpretive source materials in connection with a chosen enterprise or study, and also how to use this effectively so as to deepen and enrich the meanings connected with this activity and to make it a significant part of the larger Kingdom enterprise. He will also need to know how to guide the members of the group to sources where they can find these materials for themselves.

7. He will need to learn how to lead on from present and immediate interests to more permanent interests on a higher level; at times to lift certain group and individual needs to a level of consciousness; and to lead on from present activities to a consideration of their deeper and more significant implications. And this he should learn how to do without seeming to moralize.

8. He will need to meet the puzzling questions boys and girls ask and to supply the kind of guidance which sends them to satisfactory sources in search of the answers to their own questions. And this should be done in such a way that it will not result in minds closed to any further light which may come to them as they grow older. This implies, of course, that the leader

should have arrived at, or should be approaching, an adequate Christian philosophy of life for himself.

9. He will need to use the art of personal counseling in dealing with the difficult adjustments which individual boys and girls have to make at home, at school, in their social life. And this he will seek to do in a sympathetic but in an objective fashion.

10. On many occasions he will need to stand as a protective barrier between early adolescent youth and adults in the church who see only the blundering mistakes of these boys and girls, and fail to see the purposes and intents which lie back of them and are worthy of appreciation.

11. He will need to guide a group into frank and objective evaluation of their own enterprises, of their purposes, their attitudes, their successes, and their failures.

Securing Pioneer Leadership

" But where can we find leaders qualified to do all these many things? " asks the inquiring superintendent. The answer is by no means simple.

Is it sometimes true that a church occasionally fails to secure adequate leadership, *not* because its demands are too high and too exacting, but because its standards are not high enough to challenge the best prepared and equipped personal leadership of a community? Sometimes a community's most able leaders are not secured for the church's program because it is not educationally challenging enough to command their interest and their respect. Intelligent, resourceful people are not especially interested in volunteering for work in a Church School when they realize that it means follow-

ing along in an old traditional " rut " or following the
path of least resistance.

Churches in the midst of a transient, shifting popu-
lation have an especially difficult time in securing and
holding leaders. In such churches there needs to be a
continuous search for new people in the community
who have educational background and Christian personality and experience, who can be put to work in the
Church School. Some churches use an inventory card
at the beginning of each year, which is circulated to all
the members of the congregation, on which members or
prospective members are asked to check their various
skills and interests and the leadership responsibilities
and experience they have had in other parishes. In
such a way a pastor and a director of religious education may sometimes discover persons useful to the
Church School program who, because of modesty,
might never volunteer for leadership. Some churches
make the practice of discovering such useful information with regard to each person who comes into the
membership of the church either by confession of faith
or by transfer of membership. Such information is re-
corded on a card and carefully filed away for future
reference.

Education for Leadership in the Local Church

But, in the end, the most satisfactory method for
securing adequate leadership in the average church is
to have a continuous program of leadership education
carried on through the years, so that the church young
people themselves grow into places of responsibility
and are continually adding to their educational skill
and understanding. A staff of efficient leaders cannot

grow overnight, nor be built up in a few months or even a few years. It is a long-time process. And there is a continuous task of welding the present teaching staff into an efficient working unit, having common Christian educational ideals. The task is one of educating a group of leaders who gain such satisfaction from their work that they are built into a dependable staff, growing constantly in outlook and in ability to guide their groups efficiently.

In every local church there should be two parts to this leadership education program. One part will be to train the prospective leaders who will be ready to undertake leadership when the need arises. The other part will be to improve the effectiveness of the leaders who are already at work in the school.

Improving the Skill of the Present Teaching Staff

The following are some of the things which may be done by superintendent or supervisor to improve leadership in the Intermediate Department:

1. Observe teachers and leaders in action.

2. Observe the amount and kind of pupil participation.

3. Conduct interviews or conferences with Intermediate leaders which will result in improved group guidance and teaching techniques.

4. Stimulate the leader's desire to become more effective in group leadership and help the leader to judge his own work objectively.

5. Increase the leader's insight into such important matters as: the way personality grows; the religious implications of projects undertaken; the underlying reasons for behavior difficulties.

6. Have available for leaders resources which will supply new information when needed.

7. Help leaders to discover some of the possibilities for leadership education: within their own local church in a leadership education class; outside the local church in interdenominational leadership education schools, summer training schools, laboratory schools; through the observation of other Intermediate groups in action.

8. Help to create a working fellowship in the group of local church leaders, and the possibilities of fellowship with leaders of other churches.

9. Help the group to build standards for their own department toward which to work.

10. Provide for the leaders of the department inspiration and an adequate incentive, making clear to them the relationship of their leadership responsibility and the building of the Kingdom of God on earth.

The Workers' Departmental Conference

One of the most effective means for improving the quality of group leadership in the Intermediate Department, if wisely handled, is the departmental conference. The time in these sessions should be safeguarded from the encroachment of too many details. At least part of the time should be given to educational problems. The following are some of the matters which may be made the center of attention in such a conference:

1. Discussion of practical ways of getting at the needs, interests, concepts, and attitudes of the group, or of discovering underlying reasons for behavior difficulties of individuals who are causing trouble; perhaps

the studying together of the results of some check list or test which has been given, and planning ways for building upon the knowledge gained.

2. The occasional bringing in of an expert in the field of personal counseling and mental hygiene.

3. Discussion of objectives for the department, both general and immediate desired outcomes for the next month or quarter, based upon definite needs.

4. The review and discussion of the next unit or units to be used within the department. (See pages 81–86 for suggestions for this study.)

5. The occasional review of a book dealing with a religious point of view or with guidance in special teaching techniques.

6. The developing of standards for the department and the rating of the department according to these standards.

7. A joint conference of parents and teachers in which problems common to both are discussed and plans for co-operative effort considered.

8. A conference with leaders of other character-building agencies in the community who work with the junior high school age group.

9. A consideration of the use of the Bible in the department and how the teaching of it may be vitalized.

But the Intermediate superintendent should not consider his responsibility to his leaders ended when he has planned and carried through a series of departmental conferences. He will find that personal conferences of an informal nature will prove even more effective for those who need special help. He will see to it that his teachers have opportunities to visit other leaders at work. He will make available for them books in the field of Christian education. He will also do all in his power to encourage leaders to attend denominational and interdenominational leadership education schools, or classes carried on in the church or community, and the training schools and laboratory schools conducted by denominational boards and state and international councils during the summer months.

Parents as Potential Leaders

It is important that parents understand the changing role they should play in the lives of their growing boys and girls. They should rejoice in their children's growing independence and in their increasing ability to make wise choices for themselves. They should realize that " psychological weaning " is an important process which must be accomplished if their children are to attain emotional as well as physical maturity. As the circle of friends outside the home widens and the influence of " the crowd " comes to have more and more weight, parents should resolutely face the fact of their waning external authority over their children and rely more and more upon friendly counsel and guidance to attain their ends.

In this role of guidance, both parent and religious leader may share. Each may help and supplement the efforts of the other. It is not enough that a group of church leaders shall plan a program and then depend upon the parents to put pressure to bear at home to enforce participation in it. Both parents and leaders should consider jointly the welfare of the boys and girls they are so much interested in and together make plans for their educational and religious guidance.

To accomplish these ends, parent-teacher conferences are helpful. Occasionally also the Intermediates may wish to entertain their parents in their Church School department. These occasions may be arranged in such a way that they result in an increased understanding between parents and their children, and between parents and teachers.

Rating Myself as a Teacher

A very worth-while but searching means of growth is through measuring oneself by some standard to discover at what points one falls short. The following self-rating scale for church workers has been developed by the International Council of Religious Education. It is for the purpose of stimulating Christian leaders to further growth in personal living and in leadership ability.

SELF-RATING SCALE FOR CHURCH WORKERS

Rate yourself on each item by placing a check (✓) in the appropriate column at the right: Column 1 — not at all successful; column 2 — only slightly successful; column 3 — somewhat successful; column 4 — largely successful; column 5 — very largely successful. Keep in mind that it is not expected that you will rate yourself at the top on every point.

Personal Life	1	2	3	4	5
1. Making my everyday attitudes and conduct worthy of respect and emulation by my group.					
2. Regularly setting aside some of my time and using a wide range of resources for devotional					

Personal Life	1	2	3	4	5

reading, silent medita-
tion, and prayer.

3. Showing my group by
personal example a way
of facing current ethi-
cal issues which is heroic
in the Christian sense.

4. Making my loyalty to
the Church and its cause
an example for those
with whom I work.

5. Identifying myself with
people who are in need,
sharing their disabilities
and working to improve
their status.

6. Examining my work fre-
quently, using various
tests to discover how far
it is Christian in motive
and method.

Preparation for My Task

7. Reading books, maga-
zines, and newspapers
regularly, in order to enrich my knowledge and
to gather appropriate
materials for use in my
work.

8. Getting an understand-
ing of my task by per-
sonal conferences with
leaders, visits to other
groups who are doing
successful work, keeping
a written record of what
happens at my group

Preparation for My Task	1	2	3	4	5

meetings and checking this periodically.

9. Attending institutes, conferences, conventions, training schools, and camps wherever possible, and trying to relate what happened there to the improvement of my work.

10. Preparing carefully for every meeting of my group by defining the aims of the meeting and listing the things we might do to realize these aims.

11. Increasing my knowledge of the historical facts and the principles of life which the Bible offers.

12. Through meditation and prayer, going over my plans, trying to bring them into harmony with the purposes of God.

Personal Relationship to Group

13. Cultivating personal acquaintance with those whom I serve.

14. Building up a knowledge of the life of those whom I serve, through such means as: visiting in their homes, visiting their schools, getting ac-

Personal Relationship to Groups	1	2	3	4	5
quainted with their leisure-time interests and activities, observing them in informal contacts.					
15. Through study and experience, becoming more helpful to members of my group in meeting their personal problems.					
16. Sharing increasingly the life of my group, learning from them, and acting as a guide in their learning.					

Use of Physical Facilities

17. Making the best possible use of physical facilities.
18. Seeking in my reading, in contact with leaders, and by visiting other groups, suggestions for the improvement of the equipment used by my group.
19. Making the physical environment of my leadership beautiful and conducive to the best educational work.
20. Consulting frequently with other leaders whose work is similar to mine and taking their ideas and plans into account in my own work.
21. Studying the programs

Use of Physical Facilities	1	2	3	4	5

of all the organizations of the church that have an effect on those whom I serve, and planning my program to avoid duplication or competition.

22. Consistently seeking the counsel of my pastor and other leaders in my church with the purpose of relating my program to the general program of the congregation.

23. Taking into account in the planning of my work the suggestions and programs of educational agencies, such as the city or county council of religious education, the board of education of my denomination, et cetera.

Leadership Procedures [6]

24T. Using language readily understood by my pupils.

25T. Relating the discussions and other activities of my pupils definitely to their daily and to their crucial concerns.

26T. Having my pupils share increasingly in deciding

[6] Items 24T–30T refer particularly to teachers and other similar group leaders. Items 24W–30W are for all other workers.

Leadership Procedures	1	2	3	4	5

what the group is to do and how its purposes are to be achieved.

27T. Encouraging more friendly attitudes on the part of my pupils toward one another and toward me.

28T. Leading my pupils to work with me and with one another more readily.

29T. Leading my pupils to consult with me more easily about their personal problems or to bring their confidences to me.

30T. Leading my pupils to take part more willingly and capably in the work of the group.

24W. Making thorough advance preparation for all duties such as conducting a workers' conference or interviewing a co-worker.

25W. Using commendation wherever merited in order to recognize achievement and to give encouragement.

26W. Finding, and making available regularly to co-workers, definite sources of help and definite suggestions for im-

Leadership Procedures	1	2	3	4	5

proving the program of the church.

27W. Making co-operation easy by seeking and using suggestions from others as well as giving them.

28W. Helping, guiding, and inspiring other workers to discover their own solutions to problems rather than merely giving them mine.

29W. Depending increasingly upon consultation and counsel, rather than authority, for accomplishing desired ends.

30W. Always regarding the spiritual and ethical growth of persons as more important than the success of an organization or an institution.

Results of Leadership

31. Leading the members of my group to become more Christian in their disposition and daily conduct.

32. Leading them to grow in their personal relationship to God.

33. Leading them to become increasingly interested in studying their social environment, including

Results of Leadership	1	2	3	4	5
their immediate environment and the world at large, in an endeavor to improve it.					
34. Leading them to see more values in the Bible and to use it more consistently in Christian life.					
35. Leading them to become increasingly interested in sharing the life and work of the church.					

Lest any Intermediate leader be daunted by the difficult requirements and the high standards set for Christian leadership, it is well to bear in mind the truth that the resolute facing of personal limitations may become a challenge — a challenge to move forward along the road to vital personality growth and spiritual achievement. And, along this road, however difficult it may be, we may be sure to find divine comradeship and guidance with Him who took " the hard way." And we may have the consciousness that we are truly " God's fellow-workers."

Suggestions for Further Reading and Study

Brown, Jeanette Perkins, " Teacher Training Primer." International Council of Religious Education.

Elliott, Grace L., " Understanding the Adolescent Girl," especially the last chapter. Henry Holt and Company, Inc., 1930.

Forsythe, N. F., " Handbook for Leaders of Young People in the Local Church." Board of Education, Methodist Church.

McKibben, Frank M., " Intermediate Method in the Church School," Chapter 13. The Abingdon Press, 1926.

" Enlisting and Developing Church Workers." Bulletin No. 507. International Council of Religious Education, 1936.

" Growth in Christian Service: Suggested Pathways to More Effective Service in the Christian Cause." International Council of Religious Education, 1937.

" The Church's Opportunity in Family and Parent Education." Service Bulletin No. 420. International Council of Religious Education.

" The First Series Courses of the Leadership Training Curriculum." Bulletin No. 501. (Lists the more elementary courses.) International Council of Religious Education, 1938.

" The Second Series Courses of the Leadership Training Curriculum." Bulletin No. 502. (Lists the more advanced courses.) International Council of Religious Education, 1938.

Chapter IX

ORGANIZING THE DEPARTMENT
AND CLASS GROUP

" But the trouble in our church is that we are so poorly organized. Juniors, Intermediates, and Seniors are all mixed together. And nobody seems to know whose responsibility it is to get things straightened out."

Such complaints as this are frequently heard in workers' conferences or leadership education classes.

Or perhaps your difficulty is that there are already *too many* organizations in your local church, each competing with the other in an attempt to win the loyalty of the same boys and girls to its program and often duplicating efforts.

If either of these seems to be a real difficulty in your church, try describing or making a chart of your present organizational plan, listing the various organizations and the ages and grades included in each one of these.

Write to the leaders of your denominational board asking for their plan for the organization of an Intermediate Department in the church. Compare your present setup with their plan. At what points do you consider your church plan weak?

Local Church Situations

The organizational setup, so far as Intermediates are concerned, varies in local churches according to the number of Intermediates, the available rooms and physical facilities, the amount of leadership, and the educational vision of the church. In some small churches there may not be enough boys and girls of junior high school age to form a class. Stragglers of this age group are found in classes of juniors or in the high school or young people's class. They may act as assistants in various ways in the Church School because there is no group into which they readily fit. In other smaller churches there may be one class of Intermediates meeting with the older groups for a combined worship service in the auditorium of the church in the morning and meeting either with the junior society or with the young people's society in the evening. Or there may be, when limited facilities make it necessary, a combined Junior-Intermediate Department or a combined Intermediate-Senior Department, meeting in a separate room. In other churches having a fairly adequate educational plant, with separate departmental rooms and classrooms, there are distinct and separate departments for Intermediates. All these types of situations must be held in mind in considering organizational plans for the Intermediates in a local church.

The Purpose of Organization

A group of about thirty Intermediates in a certain local church met with their director and a guest leader to discuss plans for organizing a Pioneer Department. They were particularly concerned with plans for an hour on "family church night" which they were to spend together as a group while the adults and young people were having their various classes. It soon appeared, however, that several of the older girls in the group were eager to form a new organization for this midweek occasion, without taking into consideration the existing organizations in the Church School classes and department meeting on Sunday morning. It was not difficult to conjecture what lay back of this desire so vociferously expressed. Herein lay the possibility of new offices to which they might be elected.

It is very easy for junior high school folks who are enthusiastic for elections and enjoy holding offices to plan with their leaders complex organizations with too many officers and standing committees, and then discover that there is very little for these officers and committees to do. In an efficient organization each officer or committee should have some real function to perform and then should be held responsible by the group for the performance of it.

Book Six of the " Curriculum Guide " says [1]:

"Organization is the vehicle which carries the program toward its goal. It provides the machinery for co-operative effort on the part of persons. It is not itself the goal, but is the means of achieving the goal. Organization in the church exists for the sake of the Christian religion, not for its own sake. Whenever it becomes an end in itself, it no longer justifies its existence. If it fails to carry its load, it has itself become a load."

Questions to Ask About an Organization

Five important questions should be asked about any organization within the church which is to carry forward a wholesome Christian program and be the me-

[1] "The Organization and Administration of Christian Education in the Local Church." Book Six of The International Curriculum Guide, page 27. International Council of Religious Education, 1935. Used by permission.

dium through which a Christian group life is to function:

1. Is it as *simple* as possible to accomplish the work planned? An organization should not be formed until some need for it has arisen, and then should be only as complex as is essential for its effective functioning. Its measure of complexity will not depend so much upon the separate groups within the department as upon the existence of specific tasks to be performed without duplication of the work of other groups. Too often the demand for organization arises before the work of the group has been outlined sufficiently to determine what sort of organization would be most effective in carrying out the work proposed.

2. Is the organization *flexible* enough to meet the changing needs and interests of adolescent boys and girls? This does not mean that it should be in such constant flux that it will encourage an opportunistic type of program, with no enterprises brought to a successful termination and with no officer or committee member holding his office long enough to learn the duties and demands connected with it.

3. Is the organization *democratic?* Is there opportunity for individual choice and responsibility?

4. Does the organization have an *organic relationship to the organization of the local church as a whole?* Are those who make up the organization conscious of their responsibility to work toward the achieving of the central purpose of the church, and do they expect to receive the supervision of the whole church as it administers its program? Does each class, club, or society have an organic relation to the department as a whole, and is it conscious of its purpose and does it seek

to achieve its goals? Within the total unit of the local church or within the Intermediate Department no group should be independent of the whole.

5. Does the organization provide opportunities for Intermediates to grow in leadership ability by serving on committees, presiding at meetings, and conducting worship services under adult guidance?

Organizational Plans [2]

Basically, most churches with any sort of organizational setup for Intermediates will be following either the correlated or the unified plan or some variation of them.

The Unified Plan: According to the unified plan, all boys and girls of the church constituency from twelve to fourteen years of age or in the seventh, eighth, and ninth grades in the public school form the Intermediate Department of the local church. Their constitution is built for this departmental organization of the church. This Intermediate Department of the church carries the program of the Sunday Church School, the society meeting, the weekday session, any missionary organizations which formerly functioned, and any clubs which may be meeting during the week. The department meets Sunday morning for its Church School sessions and assembly. It meets Sunday evening in its society meeting. It meets during the week for its various club and weekday activities. It has its officers and committees responsible for the program as a whole. To provide for individual initiative, and for the fol-

[2] Compare "Pioneers on Kingdom Trails." The Manual. The Young People's Division, Executive Committee of Religious Education and Publication, Presbyterian Church, U. S., Richmond, Virginia.

lowing up of special interests growing out of the program, it may have special interest groups meeting for a period of time.

In the simplest form, this department would elect one set of officers for the entire department. There would be one set of committees, each assuming responsibility for one phase of the departmental program. But in some churches it may be necessary to set up suborganizations within the department. For example, when boys' and girls' groups meet in separate session during the week, each of these would need its own officers who would, in turn, be represented in the departmental organization.

The following chart represents graphically the unified plan:

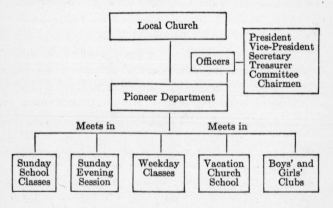

The Correlated Plan: In churches where traditions and loyalties to well-established organizations for boys and girls are especially strong, perhaps the first step might be in the direction of some correlated plan which maintains the integrity of existing organizations, but unites them in a co-operative relationship in which they may view their tasks together.

According to this plan, each class, society group, or other small unit is organized with its officers. These officers or representatives from these smaller organizations form a part of an Intermediate Cabinet or Council. Together with departmental superintendent, selected teachers, and other delegated adult leaders, they make up this representative council. An Intermediate may be elected chairman and another secretary of this cabinet. The cabinet meets at the call of the adult adviser and the chairman, and takes up matters of concern to the different groups represented or to the department as a whole. Intermediate Christian Endeavor societies, Pioneer Club groups, Weekday Church School classes (when these are denominational), and other groups for this age in the church should have representation on this cabinet. This cabinet should, in turn, be represented on the Committee or Board of Christian Education of the local church. The following chart represents graphically this type of organizational setup:

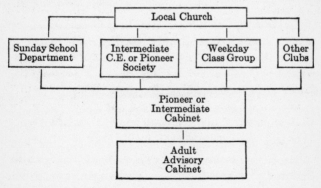

The Christian Commonwealth

A very interesting experiment in organization for the Pioneer age group is to be found in " The Christian Commonwealth " plan carried on in one of the Chicago churches.[3] It represents an attempt to approximate the reality of community life, with its complexities, and to prepare boys and girls to take their places in their own local communities.

The Commonwealth has for its motto, " Each for all, and all for each." The department is divided into three groups: " the State," " the Guilds," and " the Church." Or, rather, each member acts in three capacities, as a member of each of these three. The State has for officers a governor, lieutenant governor, secretary of state, treasurer, commissary, and sergeant at arms. The State meets on Sunday morning and then breaks up into different professional or vocational groups such as bankers, medical group, law group. The aim of the Guilds is to develop creative individuals. Each person selects the group he would like to join. He may belong to a newspaper guild, responsible for getting out a newssheet every month; a dramatic guild; artisans' or handicraft guild; artists' guild; or singers' guild. The Guilds usually meet sometime during the week. The third division of the Commonwealth is the Church. Its purpose is to " promote the ideals of Jesus throughout the whole Commonwealth." A committee, called the Clergy, plans and conducts the Sunday morning departmental worship service. Each person in the Commonwealth, then, has to act and to

[3] Hyde Park United Church, Chicago, Illinois. Dr. Douglas Horton is its originator.

exercise initiative in three different functions, as a member of the State, as a member of a Guild, and as a member of the Church.

Improving Your Organization

But perhaps you belong to a church where there is neither correlated nor unified nor, in fact, any other kind of organization in the church as a whole for Intermediates. Your department or class is a law unto itself. You do not have meetings with other counselors. You carry out your own program without considering what the others are doing. Or, you may be in the midst of a situation such as the following:

When Rev. Mr. White came to the Pleasant Valley parish, he found a mixed-up situation in the Church School. Everyone except the children under seven or eight years of age met in the church auditorium for Sunday School. There was an adult Bible class into which everyone graduated who could no longer lay claim to youth. Then there was a nondescript class, held together by a popular teacher, including all the young people from twelve to twenty approximately. A class of children who had been recently promoted from the downstairs department had seats up in front. Aside from the young people's class on Sunday morning, which some boys and girls of Intermediate age occasionally attended, there was nothing in the church for those of junior high school age except the morning service, which some of them were required by their parents to attend.

A quiet survey by the new pastor revealed the fact that there were at least a dozen boys and girls in the parish in the last two grades of grammar school.

Three of these who had just entered the seventh grade were still in the junior class down in the front seats and getting more restless and harder to manage every Sunday. The rest, when they came, sidled into the seats back of the young folks but the teacher found it difficult to hold their attention. Most of them were rarely in Sunday School. They felt that there was no place for them. The pastor also learned that several of the high school students had stopped coming to Sunday School because they didn't like the idea of having to be in the same class with " those youngsters."

The pastor first looked around for some leader who could take care of a group of Intermediates. Then one afternoon the twelve who were in the seventh and eighth grades were invited to meet the pastor and the new leader at the church for a social time. In the course of the afternoon suggestions were given as to some interesting things this group might do together — things too grown-up for juniors and of little interest to high school folks. Soon there was another corner in the church auditorium being occupied by these Intermediates, with the new leader whom the pastor had secured. Their interest had increased to such a point that they were planning to meet late in the afternoon also, to discuss and do things together which they were not able to do in the crowded room on Sunday morning. The group grew in interest and numbers. The members formed a junior choir and made a real contribution to the morning service. Because it was a small and homogeneous group, the form of organization was very simple. There was a chairman for the Sunday School class on Sunday morning, another for the evening meeting, and a third in charge of junior choir ac-

tivities.   Later the members of the group formed a
Girl Scout troop, which brought in some other girls
from nonchurch families, but the nucleus remained the
same.   Now the pastor is working out some plan
whereby this lively group of potential church leaders
shall be tied up more closely to the local church organization.   Had it not been for the farsighted pastor, the
members of this group might have been practically lost
to the church.   But now that a real place has been
found for them, they are growing in their ability and
desire to serve.   Just this last summer they helped
the pastor to carry on a Vacation Church School.

All too often, when the grading and the organization
of a Church School has been neglected, the Intermediates will be found mixed in with older and younger
folks to the intense dissatisfaction of all parties concerned.   Even in a small church they need a place of
their own in order to achieve a sense of belonging.

The Size of Classes

"How large should Intermediate classes be?" is the
question asked frequently in workers' conferences.
And a second one follows: "Should the classes be made
up of boys and girls together, or should boys and girls
be separated?"

While there seems to be a trend toward larger class
units in the Church School, there are usually several
factors which need to be taken into consideration in
each local situation before an answer can be given.
The first of these factors is the availability of the right
kind of leadership.   As W. Dyer Blair [4] says:

[4] Blair, W. Dyer, "The New Vacation Church School."
Harper & Brothers, 1934.   Used by permission.

"It is far more satisfactory to have well-trained teachers with helpers lead large groups than to multiply the number of smaller classes with poorly trained teachers."

The second factor to consider is the space available in the Church School building. If there must be a choice between four or five classes, of half a dozen pupils each, located in different corners of a room or having only " church pew " facilities, and a larger group of pupils, twenty-five to thirty, in a separate room of their own with a superior teacher and several assistants, the balance would stand in favor of the larger group, meeting together under efficient leadership and breaking up into smaller groups occasionally for committee work. Some churches are putting boys and girls together in the same class and finding that it works out successfully. The success of this venture will probably depend somewhat upon the amount of group spirit and the number of interests that the boys and girls share. There is a wholesome give-and-take in a well-managed junior high school home room which is mutually helpful to both boys and girls. There is no reason why a similar tradition may not be built up also in a Church School department.

Organization of a Class Group

The organization of each class should be very simple. There should be only enough to carry forward the work of the class and to insure the class's representation in the departmental organization. A class chairman, secretary-treasurer, and whatever temporary committees are needed to take care of specific responsibilities may be appointed or elected. In some cases the class chairman may represent the class in the Departmental

Council. In other cases the class representative may be another person chosen by the class. The larger the class unit, the more certain phases of the class activity will need to be delegated to committees who, with an assistant, may carry on their investigations or the forming of their plans, and report back to the larger group.

Grading in the Pioneer Department

The matter of grading in the Pioneer Department requires an unusual amount of discernment and tact. The one who carries the responsibility for the placement of pupils in classes, and for their promotion from one department to another, should have constantly in mind that the central issue is the growth of Christian personality. If it is true, as the experience of many leaders seems to indicate, that more worth-while changes are wrought in character and personality when pupils' backgrounds are similar, then pupils should be helped to find their way into Church School groups in which they will have a real sense of belonging because there is not too much feeling of difference between themselves and their associates. This suggests that Church School leaders will constantly be working to build up natural groupings within a department.

Mr. Dimock, in his investigations into the interests and activities of two hundred boys,[5] found that they were more apt to be regular in attendance, to participate more fully in the program and be more keenly interested in it, and to become more permanent members of the group when they were enrolled in groups

[5] Dimock, Hedley S., " Rediscovering the Adolescent." Association Press, 1937.

with a fairly high friendship index. On the other hand, boys who belonged to groups which were really heterogeneous collections of individuals, held together only by the fact of similar age or grade, with a low degree of cohesiveness, were very apt to be irregular in attendance, spasmodic in interest, and ready to drop out when something else held a greater appeal. Perhaps, in some cases, we should be less conscientious about keeping all those of the same age and grade together in one unit, and more concerned that boys and girls have the chance in Church School to be with their "crowd," or with those of the same sociological grouping.

Promotion from One Department to Another

Another important question is, When and under what conditions should Intermediates or Pioneers be considered ready for promotion to the Senior Department? Should certain standards be reached before such promotion takes place, as in public school? Or should pupils be passed on regularly with their promotion to the tenth grade in high school or on arriving at the fifteenth birthday?

Some departments require that a certain amount of memorization shall be completed before pupils are considered ready to graduate from the department. This requirement occasionally causes difficulties and embarrassment to those concerned. But whatever standards for achievement are set up, they should be arrived at with due consideration of the objectives of the departmental program.

In this connection, especially with early adolescents, it is important that the chief consideration shall always be what is best for the personality growth of the individuals concerned, and not what is most convenient administratively. At the same time, a record for consistency should be maintained, so that there may be no chance of an accusation of favoritism or injustice on the part of adult leaders by the pupils.

Suggestions for Further Reading and Study

Brown, Elizabeth, "Intermediate Department Handbook." General Board of Christian Education, Methodist Episcopal Church, South, Nashville, Tennessee, 1936.

Desjardins, Lucile, " The Pioneer Department of the Church." The Judson Press, 1936.

McKibben, Frank M., "Intermediate Method in the Church School," Part III. The Abingdon Press, 1926.

" A Manual for Leaders of Intermediates," pages 29–40. Christian Board of Publication, St. Louis, Missouri, 1937.

"Pioneers on Kingdom Trails." The Manual. The Young People's Division, Executive Committee of Religious Education and Publication, Presbyterian Church, U. S., Richmond, Virginia.

CHAPTER X

PROVIDING A PHYSICAL ENVIRONMENT FOR WORK AND WORSHIP

"BUT what can we do when our classes must sit in pews with a dozen other classes seated in close proximity and each competing with the others in making the most noise?" asks one despairing teacher.

"And how can you expect boys and girls to worship on Sunday in the same gymnasium where they have been playing basketball during the week?" asks another.

"And how can you expect boys and girls to get into an attitude of study when none of the work and study tools are available, such as blackboards, tables, pencils, dictionaries, et cetera?" says a despairing third.

It sometimes seems as though the most worthy motives, the most carefully planned curriculum, the most carefully selected and trained leadership can hardly offset the physical environment in which boys and girls are placed on Sunday morning for their one hour of Christian education a week.

Places Where Intermediates Meet

In a certain large city church a new educational building has recently been dedicated and opened for use. In this building the Intermediate Department has an assembly room, with separate classrooms leading off from it. In the front of this assembly room is a beautiful altar, a memorial gift. There is a sweet-

172

toned piano in the room and several well-selected religious pictures are hung on the side walls. Each separate classroom is equipped with a table, chairs, a blackboard, maps, and a place for a shelf of books. A cabinet in one corner holds the supplies.

In another church a large basement room has recently been remodeled into an attractive chapel, with fairly large classrooms leading from it. This combined chapel and departmental room must serve a combined Junior-Intermediate Department, because of a limitation of space in the Church School building. In the six classrooms combined classes of boys and girls in the fourth, fifth, sixth, seventh, and eighth grades hold their class sessions. The two smaller rooms are to serve, the one as a library and the other as a committee room or a workroom. To these rooms individuals or committees may go for special investigation or reference or project work under the guidance of an assistant leader.

Still another church is not so fortunately situated so far as its Intermediates are concerned, for they are forced to meet in a basement gymnasium. It is a bare, unattractive room. The chairs scrape on the floor. There is no place to hang pictures. The leaders wonder sometimes why it is so difficult to obtain an atmosphere of worship on Sunday morning.

In another church the Intermediates must occupy seats in the church auditorium along with the Seniors and the Adults. For worship service they sit on the right-hand side of the room according to their classes. Either their class sessions must be held in these same pews, with their teacher standing in front of them, or they may find some corners in the church where they can crowd together in an irregular circle, or in the summer meet out of doors in the shade.

It is evident that there are many different situations in which Pioneer leaders must carry on their work. Nor can it be said that the best teaching is always to be found in the Church School with superior equipment and housing facilities. To be sure, adequate equipment is decidedly an asset to good teaching. But in many small churches with limited financial resources and meager equipment, teachers are to be found who are resourceful enough to make the most of whatever they have in the way of equipment. A corner of a church auditorium, screened off from the rest, may occasionally become a place where more vital Christian learning goes on than that in some luxurious clubroom in which idle boys or girls fool around during a class session with no teacher or with one who is very inadequate.

Mildred Hewitt says [1]:

" The right physical setting for a Church School depends not so much on the amount of money spent as it does on such qualities as imagination and ingenuity; imagination to picture the kind of environment needed, and ingenuity to produce that environment out of the available resources."

An Ideal for an Intermediate Department

Ideal housing and physical equipment for carrying on the various activities suggested in this textbook would include the following types of rooms for various occasions:

1. A room suitable for the more formal departmen-

[1] Hewitt, Mildred, " The Church School Comes to Life," page 145. The Macmillan Company, 1932. Used by permission.

tal worship service on Sunday morning. This room should be attractive, with some beauty spot or symbolic emblem as a center upon which to focus attention during worship. This may be an altar, a worship screen, a beautiful religious picture, or merely a table or pulpit with a Bible or some other appropriate symbol arranged upon it. The chairs should be arranged either in straight rows, with an aisle in the middle, or in a semicircular formation. There should be a well-tuned piano.

In some churches the Intermediates may be allowed the use of the church sanctuary for their own period of departmental worship. In other churches a youth or children's chapel may be used for this worship service. By carefully planning a schedule with other departmental groups, a chapel may be made available for several groups in the course of the morning. In one church the Intermediates have made for themselves a beautiful copper altar, with a cross in the center, which has helped to beautify their room.

2. In addition to a room adapted for worship, there should be classrooms set up informally for discussion and study groups. A good arrangement, if the class is not too large, is to have the chairs arranged around a table. For these discussion and work periods a blackboard is almost indispensable. When separate rooms are an impossibility, the corners of a larger room may be separated from each other by the use of screens. These screens may be constructed with a blackboard attached to the inner side, so that they serve a double purpose. Even in the auditorium of some churches such blackboard screens may be used, and folded up and packed away when the Sunday School session is

over. The separating of class groups in such a way, while it does not shut off the noise, nevertheless shuts away some of the distracting views, and thus helps to improve the educational situation.

3. Conferences and discussions on interesting and important questions should quicken the desire on the part of pupils for further study and investigation. Materials for such study should be provided, and also a place where boys and girls can carry on their investigations without too much interruption. A browsing table or a library nook, with a table near by on which to write, will often prove sufficient for this purpose and will afford a worklike atmosphere for a departmental room. Some large churches are fortunate enough to have a library of carefully selected books from which leaders may select books for particular units. In some churches, if the pastor's study is in the parish house and conveniently located, he may, in co-operation with a leader, arrange a shelf of books especially helpful in developing some particular course of study. Public libraries, upon the request of a responsible person, will frequently arrange an extension loan of books on special subjects for a period of weeks. A Bible dictionary, a Bible concordance, and a Bible atlas should always be available for use by junior high school pupils.

4. A workshop where manual activities and various handicraft pursuits may be carried on is an excellent room to have in the church basement for Intermediate boys and girls. In one small church in a community where there was no recreational center, a group of enterprising young people proposed cleaning out the debris which had been accumulating underneath the

church in a section adjoining the furnace room, and making it over into a workshop and game room.

5. For churches able to afford it, an excellent addition to educational and recreational equipment is a stage fitted with lights, curtains, and other equipment for amateur dramatics. There should also be a storeroom or chest for storing away various sorts of costumes between plays.

Some room or corner in the church, at least, the Intermediates ought to be able to call their own, and they should be held responsible for keeping this in good condition. Sometimes when they have had a real share in providing or paying for the furnishing and equipment, their pride in their own room results in increased thoughtfulness and care to keep it looking neat and attractive. Occasionally Intermediates have been allowed to redecorate their room and to arrange it according to their own ideas. Sometimes in these ways they have first experienced that feeling of responsible ownership or trusteeship which will help them to consider themselves custodians or guardians of church property.

Making One Room Do

Where there is no possibility of elaborate equipment, the one room may be made to serve all purposes by using a little ingenuity. Many interesting attempts have been made to build worship screens of three panels of composition board, hinged together. Such a screen, when completed, may be set up in front for a worship service and then folded up and put away during the week, when the same room must be used for other purposes. The three panels may be carved,

Gothic fashion, and stained or painted a dark color. Sometimes a cross or some other religious symbol may be carved in the central panel, or a beautiful religious picture may be framed in it, or a length of deep, rich red or blue fabric may be hung on the bare wall in the front of a room and a picture placed on this background. A plain table, with good lines, placed in front of this, with an open Bible, a cross, or some candles or flowers, will add to the atmosphere of the room and will help to create desirable worship attitudes. The one who is responsible for arranging the room should study the possibilities of each wall space and arrange the room so as to gain the most favorable setting, making sure that the members of the group are not forced to face glaring light from windows in front.

Tables for work may be at the back of this room and the class sessions may be carried on around these tables, with screens to separate the classes.

A bulletin board is a useful piece of equipment in an assembly room or classroom, and may be made by boys in the department who are taking manual training in public school. On this bulletin board pictures, clippings, news items, exhibits, or handwork pertinent to the unit may all be placed from time to time by pupils or teachers. On it also may be placed announcements of interest to the department, directions for work, and rules formulated by the group for the conduct of the department. There should also be shelves or a supply closet where hymnals, Bibles, and other books and work materials may be stored away neatly when not in use. Good lighting, proper ventilation, freedom from outside distractions, and proper toilet arrangements should all, of course, be provided for in a well-ordered school. Essential also are comfortable seating arrangements, a supply of necessary work materials, and a place for the hanging of wraps. The pictures which hang on the wall should be very carefully selected for their religious and artistic value.

While it is understood that the Intermediates should not be given the preference in rooms over the Beginners, Primary, and Junior Departments, yet they should not be given the least desirable place in the entire church building, as so frequently happens. The attractiveness and comfort of the room assigned to them should at least equal that of the rooms in the average homes in the community.

Records for the Intermediate Department

The secretary of the Intermediate Department has an important function to perform, for the records of a Church School are a vital help in planning for the future program. If these records are complete enough, they may suggest in a very tangible way the points of strength and weakness or of success and failure in this program. There are various kinds of reports which have proved useful in an Intermediate Department:

Attendance records: These inform the leaders of a department and a school what percentage of the enrollment and of the potential constituency is taking advantage of the program set up. Irregularity in class attendance should make leaders alert to discover the causes. Only as these underlying causes are remedied may constructive work be done in building up the Pioneer Department. Contests which result in increased attendance for a few Sundays are by no means a permanent solution. A convenient and practical form of attendance record card is Form 4B–5A in the International System of Records and Reports.

Individual pupil cumulative record: Cumulative records of individual boys and girls, in which facts and impressions from time to time are preserved, are almost essential to pupil guidance. In this individual record may be placed such items of information as: address, age, grade, information about home and family, special problems, aptitudes, needs, skills, interests or hobbies, church relationships, whatever religious ideas and attitudes have been expressed, and achievement in tests, class projects, and discussions. Form 8A of the International System is designed for this use. Many teachers, however, will use a private notebook for this purpose.

Records of teachers and prospective leaders: A permanent record of every teacher who is working or has been working in the department should be kept, giving his training, his experience, and his relationship to the department. Information concerning prospective leaders should also be filed away for future reference. Form 3B1, " Leader's Registration and Permanent Record Blank," in the International System, may be used for this purpose.

A diary record for class sessions: Another important kind of record for the individual teacher to keep is a diary record, or a session-by-session running account of what actually happens in class, together with the leader's preliminary planning and his subsequent evaluation. Such a record is especially important when experimental work is being carried on in a department or when a department is developing indigenous units of study. If these records are kept from year to year, and studied carefully, a department should avoid the mistake of too frequent repetition of certain emphases and too much duplication in projects and procedures.

The logbook: An increasingly popular form of record is the record of a unit or a project which the boys and girls themselves make. This may be the work of a committee in the department or of one person or committee in a class. This kind of record may be illustrated with snapshots of groups engaged in special activities. Sometimes freehand drawing may be used. Programs of the class or department, party invitations, worship services planned by committees from the department may all be pasted in this book to help to tell the story of the year's program.

Verbatim reports: Occasionally it is a very helpful thing for a teacher to invite into his class an expert stenographer who, seated in an unobtrusive place, will take down in shorthand a complete and detailed report of the conversation or discussion which goes on in the class session. Such a detailed record of the conversation between pupils and teacher is most enlightening and may be used as the basis for an interview between supervisor and teacher. Weaknesses in teaching procedure are likely to be revealed in this type of report.

Keeping a record of the results of tests and check lists: Objective tests that have been given or interest finders that have been checked should be preserved and compared with later tests of a similar nature given to the same group. Later it may be interesting to compare, for example, the norm or average in a Biblical information test, especially if a few months of inter-

vening time have been given to " catching up " on
Biblical information.

A statistical record for the department: An accurate
statistical report for a quarter or for a year should
include such items as: the number enrolled at the beginning and at the end of the period, including teachers, pupils, and officers; the increase or decrease in
enrollment; the comparison with the previous year
at the same time; possibly comparative records with
other departments; the percentage of those enrolled in
attendance as compared with a previous period; the
amount of offering each Sunday and the average
amount per Sunday and per pupil. A statistical record
of this sort may be exhibited in graphic form so as to
be interesting and meaningful. Some artistic Pioneer
may be interested in making these graphic charts.

Reports to parents: There is a good deal of perplexity today concerning the question of whether it is wise
to send monthly or quarterly report cards to parents
according to public-school custom. Some churches
advocate this measure as a means of encouraging parents to co-operate with the Church School in regard
to home work, punctuality, and regularity of attendance. However, very serious questions arise, such as:
" For what special things shall we grade boys and girls
in the Church School? " " How can we be sure to do
them justice in our grading when we meet them for
only a brief period on Sunday? "

Some leaders suggest that they should be graded on
the basis of the amount of memory work learned, or the
questions they are able to answer, or the grades they
receive on objective tests. Others think that they
should be graded for such tangible things as bringing

their Bibles every Sunday and their Sunday attendance. Still others attempt to grade pupils for such attitudes as co-operation, reverence, and interest.

Leaders today recognize that the objectives of the Church School are much broader and include much more than the ability to memorize Bible passages and to answer questions correctly. They realize that religious education is concerned with the development of religious attitudes. But who is really capable of measuring fairly and accurately the attitudes of reverence and loyalty of boys and girls in a class? Or who can measure with justice the amount of progress any Intermediate boy or girl has made in religious living?

Many private schools and some of the more progressive public schools are discarding the old, traditional methods of exact grades for children in the various subjects. They consider it more ethical and more wholesome to measure a pupil, not in competition with his classmates, since their abilities are apt to differ so widely, but according to his own ability and the progress he has made in mastering his own faults and limitations. They are tending toward a more informal type of report to parents, in which special matters that call for the co-operation of both home and school are brought to the attention of parents. Some schools are also working toward some form of achievement chart which teacher and pupils may work on together, so that grading really becomes a co-operative affair carried on in a personal interview in which the two feel free to talk over together in a friendly way any special skills or attitudes which should be achieved and which are essential for further progress. Such an informal method, however, demands a friendly relationship between pupil and teacher, and a clear understanding of home and parental attitudes.

Suggestions for Further Reading and Study

Blair, W. Dyer, "The New Vacation Church School," pages 158–163. "Recording the Life of the School." Harper & Brothers, 1934. Used by permission.

Vieth, Paul H., "Improving Your Sunday School." The Westminster Press, 1930.

"Equipment for Intermediates," pages 116–120. "A Manual for Leaders of Intermediates." Christian Board of Publication, St. Louis, Missouri, 1937.

Research Bulletin No. 8, "Housing and Equipment for the Church School." International Council of Religious Education.

The International System of Church School Records and Reports. International Council of Religious Education.

CHAPTER XI

BUILDING TOGETHER FOR YOUTH IN THE COMMUNITY

PERHAPS you are one of the leaders who are looking at the problems and needs of younger adolescents from a community point of view. You are concerned not only with the privileged boys and girls who come from church families but also with those underprivileged pupils without church background. You are insistently asking the question, " What can the leaders of this community do together to protect boys and girls from the disintegrating influences which are threatening their moral character? "

Or perhaps you are asking the question, " How can a church ever hope to build an adequate Intermediate program when the public school and other community organizations absorb so much of the time and energy of younger adolescents? "

As a start in facing this problem, make a list of all the different agencies which are demanding the time and the loyalty of those junior high school boys and girls whom you know best. Mark a plus (+) sign next to those which you feel have a constructive, character-building program for youth. Mark with a minus (−) sign those which you feel have commercial gain as their chief end, rather than personality growth of those participating. If you are uncertain about the character-building values of any of these agencies in the life of youth, place a question mark (?) after them. Make a point to study more thoroughly the objectives and programs of these doubtful organizations.[1]

Consider also very thoughtfully and discuss with other leaders (if you are in a leadership education class) what is the distinctive function of the public school, the home, and the church in relation to the personality development and character growth of these younger adolescents.

A Desperate Need

A desperate need is making itself felt in American community life today. It is the need for the integrating of the many conflicting forces which are pulling the lives of boys and girls in different directions. If you do not feel the pressure of these conflicting forces, put yourself in the shoes of a modern boy or girl. Follow these twelve-year-olds through a day or a week in their busy schedule. Go with them to public school, back to their homes again, onto the streets, into their various clubs, into the neighborhood movies. Discover the whole gamut of contradictory ideas, impressions, and points of view which flood their minds from table talk at home, from the daily newspapers, from classroom discussions, from the movies, from community gossip on the street corners. Listen to the varying calls which come to them, " This is the way, walk ye in it." You will then realize their desperate need for wise leaders who will help to straighten out in their minds the many conflicting ideas and loyalties, and thus help to save them from mental and moral confusion. You

[1] Pendry, E. R., and Hartshorne, Hugh, in " Organizations for Youth," list all these various organizations and describe their objectives and programs. McGraw-Hill Book Company, Inc., 1935.

will wonder anew how immature persons, thrust into the midst of so many conflicting influences, can ever grow into well-poised, consistent Christian personalities.

The complexity of the forces influencing the life of youth today is in sharp contrast to the simplicity of early American life, built as it was around the three fundamental social units, the home, the church, and the school. Then too in the more homogeneous life of pioneer days the home, the church, and the school had similar points of view. But the process of the secularization of the public schools began, sectarianism increased, and communities began to be made up of homes with diverse customs, ideals, and traditions. Today over three hundred different educational, social, and recreational agencies compete for the time and the loyalty of boys and girls in this country, each of them professing idealistic concern for their welfare. As a result, boys and girls have little time for home and family duties, and no time for the church except a brief hour on Sunday morning.

The situation has become so desperate that there is a growing movement toward the co-ordination of constructive community forces, public and private, responsible for social welfare, crime prevention, and character-building. This movement is gathering momentum. These social and character-building agencies are attempting to build around childhood and youth a protective wall to save them from those destructive, commercialized agencies that do not have the welfare of growing persons at heart.

Several influences have been silently at work to bring about this uniting of forces. There has been recognition, on the part of many social and religious leaders, of the overcomplexity of the community problem and the ineffectiveness of unrelated effort. Along with this has come also an increased understanding of adolescent personality, with the conviction growing among many educators that lack of harmony and consistency among character-building agencies themselves may actually result in disintegration of character in those whom they are seeking to help.

It is plain that the task of character-building in this generation is a responsibility far too great for any one of the various competing agencies to accomplish alone.

There is a quaint old legend of a kingdom which had no palace for its king — only a desolate, waste spot, ugly and overgrown with weeds, in the heart of the city, where a beautiful palace had once stood. But when the chief musicians of the realm, encouraged and lured on by two small boys who had discovered the secret of playing together, learned to drop their jealous fears and their differences and played their lyres together in sweet harmony, then the palace rose from the ground by magic.

On a more authentic basis is the Old Testament story of the rebuilding of the walls around the city of Jerusalem, a co-operative enterprise which, according to the record, took only fifty-two days when the citizens, under the tactful and aggressive leader, Nehemiah, " had a mind to work " together. The enemies outside, who sought the city's destruction, could do nothing to prevent this building enterprise, for each man worked in his own place, " over against his own house," but in co-operation with his neighbors.

This task in our American community life to which

thoughtful citizens have set themselves is no fifty-two-day task. It is one that will confront each generation, and it demands the help of every constructive community agency. Many organizations are playing a noteworthy part in this entire enterprise. Especially helpful to boys and girls in the rural sections of our country is the 4-H Club movement. The Boy Scout and the Girl Scout movements are outstanding in their character-building programs for Intermediate boys and girls. The Camp Fire Girls' program, with the beauty of its symbolism, appeals to many adolescent girls and meets a real need in their lives. There is no space here to mention many other worthy agencies. For a description of their aims and their programs, you will wish to read " Organizations for Youth," by E. R. Pendry and Hugh Hartshorne.

But basically important still in the development of stalwart personality stand the home, the school, and the church, when they are at their best. A Christian home, providing security, intimate comradeship, and consistent guidance from the very earliest years, is still the most powerful influence in the lives of many boys and girls.

The public school is taking more and more seriously its responsibility of building good citizens. It has accepted character education as its central function.

The question remains, What is the place of the church in this total co-operative enterprise in behalf of childhood and youth?

The Church's Place in This Movement

In the midst of this movement, the Christian church must surely find its place. It cannot expect to function separately or independently of all these other agencies so concerned for youth's welfare. In the early life of the American community, the church was a dominating factor. It influenced strongly, and, in many cases, controlled the moral standards, the political practices, the economic life, the educational policies, and the plans for social welfare of the community of which it was the center. But, one by one, these responsibilities have been relinquished. However, the Christian Church still has a unique contribution to make to the lives of the young, for the heart of the message of its Founder has to do with the unique value of persons as " sons of God."

And what is this contribution? The Christian church introduces young people to God and to his sanctions for human conduct. It leads them to worship. It helps them to form worthy ideals and to develop worthy motives and convictions. It opens up to them a philosophy of life " as broad as the needs of the human soul and as deep as the resources of the Kingdom of God." It provides for them a vitalizing fellowship with those who are working at Kingdom tasks.

The Christian religion, which the Church seeks to share with the world, provides an organizing center for personality. It gives meaning to life and learning. It creates ethical standards rooted in a moral universe. It gives to youth a great, inspiring Friendship. It has within it power to transform unworthy purposes into worthy aims. It gives to youth a cause worth living and dying for.[2]

Realizing the unique contribution which the church

[2] Compare the statement of the unique contribution of the Christian religion given in the bulletin, " The Church in Co-

may make and desiring to share in any co-operative effort for the good of a community, many pastors and church leaders are honestly puzzled. They ask such questions as these: Should a local church become one of the active agencies in a co-ordinating council, on a par with the rest, perhaps having to face the possibility of compromise of its spiritual standards as a member of a co-operating group made up largely of secular agencies? Or should it take the initiative in starting such a movement even when the other churches of the community are reluctant to step forward? Should the church seek the dominating place in the affairs of such a council? Or should the influence of the church be exerted in a " mildly pervasive " way, through the influence of Christian leaders of these so-called " secular " institutions who have got their inspiration for social welfare from the Church and its message? Should the church lose its identity as an institution when it comes to these co-operative movements and rely upon the Christian influence of the leaders who have been molded by its ideals? No final answer can be given to these important questions here. But in each church and community they should be faced thoughtfully and honestly.

First Steps in Co-operation

Perhaps you are now convinced that the church and its leaders have a definite responsibility for initiating

ordination with Community Agencies," page 17. International Council of Religious Education.

See also the function of the church in " Report of the Findings Committee of the Advisory Conference of Professional Leaders of Character-building Agencies." International Council of Religious Education.

some sort of co-operative community action where there is a real need. Your next question will be: How may a group or a few interested leaders go about organizing for this purpose?

After you have been convinced of the need for such a move in your own community, your church leaders might take the initiative in calling together in an unofficial way interested leaders of youth, representing the different agencies. Or you might get in touch with a key leader in the community, such as the superintendent of schools, and persuade him to take the first step. The first meeting should be for the purpose of getting better acquainted with one another and with the programs represented. At this first meeting each person might state briefly the objectives of his organization and the special goals toward which it is working at the present time. In such a way each would become more fully aware of the values each of the others is striving for, and a sense of underlying unity might be achieved.

A close study of the respective programs of each character-building organization should help to show all the teachers that the various organizations appeal to different interests of boys and girls and that these various interests may each have their place in fashioning the personality of youth, if only leaders work together. Every professional leader should be interested in the work of other professional leaders so that he may learn to see life from the total viewpoint of youth, and in this light rethink the educational program of his organization more in harmony with the other programs that are affecting the lives of these same young people.

After the various programs have been studied, leaders may then wish to analyze their respective programs to discover points at which there is serious conflict or duplication.[3]   They should also discover whatever gaps there may be in educational experience which no community agency is providing for.   They should also look out for a certain minority group of boys and girls who may not be provided for adequately by any one of the agencies.

Concrete Examples of Co-operative Community Effort

Throughout the country there have been many interesting reports of co-operative community efforts in various centers.   In a recent national survey, 163 cities and towns in 20 different states were reported as having some organized form of community co-ordination. At times the forces particularly concerned with juvenile delinquency have fostered the movement.   At other times and in other places the public-school leaders or the church leaders have led the way.   The church has been the instigator in other situations.

In Los Angeles, a Co-ordinating Council encouraged a co-operative summer program throughout the county, with special attention given to districts having a high rate of juvenile delinquency.   In this program churches, playground centers, WPA workers, and public schools all have a part.[4]

In Madison, New Jersey, as a result of community co-operation, 25 spot maps were prepared, showing different aspects of community life.

[3] The chart found on page 54 of this text would be helpful in this connection.

[4] Compare the bulletin " Who Is Delinquent? " The Los Angeles County Plan of Co-ordinating Councils.   Rotary Club of Los Angeles, California, 1936.

In southeastern Ohio, 160 local communities and 12,000 children and young people were reached in an interdenominational vacation program developed through the Ohio Council of Religious Education.

In the year 1938 the New Jersey Christian Laymen's Commission, working in co-operation with the state council of religious education and other social welfare agencies, was responsible for 40 different summer projects throughout the state in neglected areas where the need of a constructive program for boys and girls seemed greatest.

The types of work carried on by co-ordinating councils are varied. But among the many forms of co-operative effort and achievement are the following [5]:

1. The survey of communities to discover major needs, problems, and conditions affecting the lives, particularly of children and youth.

2. The discovery of delinquency areas.

3. Increasing recreational and group facilities, such as centers, playgrounds, and so forth.

4. Removing or controlling destructive influences, such as gambling machines near schools, undesirable moving pictures, sale of liquor and tobacco to minors, the sale on magazine stands of smutty magazines.

5. The planning of a community calendar, allowing one night each week free for the churches, one night for the schools, and so forth.

Intermediate leaders, aware of the need for integration in the life of boys and girls, should be quick to see the possibilities in such united effort. They will plan their Intermediate program in the local church with

[5] Compare Beam, Kenneth S., " Co-ordinating Councils. How Shall They Be Organized? " National Probation Association, New York. Used by permission.

these community resources and influences in mind. They will be glad to share in united effort in behalf of youth.

Perhaps as we all forget the differences which divide us and learn how to " play together," we too may begin to rid our community life of the " waste, ugly spots " which threaten youth. Perhaps we too may help to build the Kingdom of God in our midst.

Suggestions for Further Reading and Study

Beam, Kenneth S., " Co-ordinating Councils. How Shall They Be Organized? " National Probation Association, New York. 10 cents.

Fiske, G. W., " Community Forces for Religious Education." Cokesbury Press, 1922.

Glover, Katherine, and Dewey, Evelyn, " Children of the New Day." D. Appleton-Century Company, 1934.

Hartshorne, Hugh, " Character in Human Relations." Charles Scribner's Sons, 1932.

Johnson, Ernest F., " The Church and Society." The Abingdon Press, 1935.

Pendry, E. R., and Hartshorne, Hugh, " Organizations for Youth." McGraw-Hill Book Company, Inc., 1935.

" The Scout Program in Protestant Churches." A Manual of Practical Procedures Related to the Program of the Church. The Protestant Committee on Scouting. 2 Park Avenue, New York, New York.

" Who Is Delinquent? " The Los Angeles County Plan of Co-ordinating Councils. Rotary Club of Los Angeles, California, 1936.

" Youth — How Communities Can Help." United States Office of Education, Superintendent of Documents, Washington, D. C., 1936.

CHAPTER XII

MEASURING PROGRESS

IT IS obviously very unfair to measure the effectiveness and excellence of the Intermediate Department in one local church against the Intermediate Departments in other churches, since too many factors enter into the situations to make them comparable. In one community other youth organizations outside the church are so strong that they compete with the church for the time and loyalty of Intermediates and make it doubly difficult to build the church program successfully. In some churches the equipment and the facilities are so poor, and the financial resources so limited, that a leader is working against serious handicaps. In still other churches the homes from which the junior high school pupils come are so widely scattered that few opportunities for midweek sessions are available. The question of leadership is much more difficult in some communities and churches than in others. Each church will be aware of its own limitations and difficulties.

A Measuring Rod

However, the following measuring rod may be helpful to you in analyzing your own situation and in discovering points of strength and weakness in the local church departmental program for younger adolescents.

Go through the following list of items carefully, placing a plus mark (+) before those which you think are carried out in your class or department. Underline those items which you propose to work on during the coming year. After you have done this, write out a thoughtful statement of definite ways in which you hope to improve either your department or your class program during the following year, referring to the various items by number.

Write down also special points in the program at which you would like additional help. List several books in the bibliographies which you wish to read.

At the end of the year, check your list once more to see what progress has been made in improving your Intermediate program.

Measuring the Effectiveness of Your Church School Program for Intermediates

1. What means have you used this year for discovering the needs, interests, attitudes, and ideas of your pupils?

Personal counseling.	( )
Visits in the homes.	( )
Conferences or exchange of reports with other leaders in community character-building agencies.	( )
Use of tests or check lists.	( )
Informal conversations with individuals in the group.	( )
Observation of pupils.	( )
Parent-teacher conferences.	( )
Reading books on adolescent psychology.	( )
————————————————	( )

2. Which of the following goals have you been seeking to realize in your class (or in your department) this year?

God-consciousness, faith in God, love toward him.	( )
Love for Jesus Christ, acceptance of him.	( )
Christlike character, Christian living.	( )
Building a Christian world — the Kingdom of God.	( )
Building a Christian philosophy of life.	( )

Commitment to the Christian Church and its program. ( )
Appreciation and understanding of the Bible and our
    religious heritage.[1] ( )

Write below three specific objectives you have been
working toward in class or department, consistent with
the objectives given above.

(1) _____
(2) _____
(3) _____

3. Is the group life within your class (or department)

Thoroughly democratic? ( )
Entirely co-operative within the group and in relation-
    ship to other groups? ( )
Such as to allow and encourage creative expression on
    the part of each member? ( )
Resulting in a widening fellowship with those outside
    their immediate circle? ( )
Such as to encourage responsibility of individuals to
    the group as a whole? ( )
Cohesive in nature with each individual feeling that he
    belongs? ( )
Such as to emphasize spiritual and social values in pref-
    erence to material profit and gain? ( )

4. To what extent are the following principles of
program-building being carried out in your department:

Is the program comprehensive? ( )
Is the program unified? ( )
Is the program well-balanced? ( )
Is the program well graded to the group? ( )
Is the program built upon the interests and needs of
    the group? ( )
Is the program planned to realize the objectives which
    have been formulated? ( )

[1] For a fuller statement of these general objectives compare
pages 47–49.

Is the program flexible enough to make opportunity
    for the changes needed without becoming oppor-
    tunistic? ( )
Does the program allow room for a variety of individ-
    ual interests and abilities and their expression? ( )

5. During the past year has each of the following
elements in a Pioneer program been emphasized?

Bible study. ( )
Study of church history, religious music, biography, et
    cetera. ( )
Discussion of personal and current social problems. ( )
Is there satisfactory worship within the department?
    within the class? Do the members of the group
    have an opportunity for training in worship? ( )
Is there some place for symbolism or ceremonialism in
    the entire program? ( )
Has evangelism, or winning a personal decision for
    Christ on the part of the pupils, a place in the
    program? ( )
Is training for church membership a part of the pro-
    gram? ( )
Are missionary education and a study of Christian mis-
    sions an integral part of the total program? ( )
Is stewardship emphasized? ( )
Are recreational and social events a part of the pro-
    gram? Are these events contributing to a whole-
    some group spirit? ( )
What service projects have been carried through satis-
    factorily this year in the class (or department)?
    Dramatic. ( )
    Constructive. ( )
    Special feature programs. ( )
    Exhibits, et cetera. ( )
    _____ ( )

6. What lesson or program materials are being used
in your Pioneer Department, in Church School classes,
in society meetings, in other parts of your program?

a. Are these published by:

Denominational agencies?   ( )
Private or nondenominational agencies?   ( )
A combination of both?   ( )

b. Are the Church School lessons

International Uniform Lessons?   ( )
Departmental or Group Graded?   ( )
Closely Graded?   ( )
Elective?   ( )
Indigenous (developed in your own group)?   ( )
A combination of these?   ( )

c. Do you use a unit

Exactly as it is written?   ( )
Do you adapt and supplement it?   ( )
Do you sometimes discard a course and use one more
    to your own liking?   ( )
Do you make your own choice of units, regardless of
    what the rest of the school is using?   ( )
Or do you co-operate with the rest of the school staff
    in the selection of courses?   ( )
Do you depend upon the Bible for your teaching, with-
    out attempting to use any lesson courses? ( )

d. Do you consider your Pioneer curriculum

Well-balanced?   ( )
Christian?   ( )
Educationally good?   ( )

e. What suggestions for change would you make?

7. Which of the following class procedures have you used within the last six months?

Lecture method.   ( )
Group discussion.   ( )
Project.   ( )
Storytelling.   ( )
Use of pictures and other visual aids.   ( )
Informal conversation on problems of current interest
    to the group.   ( )

Use of check lists or tests.   ( )
Planning worship services.   ( )
Reports on committee work or individual research.   ( )
An activity period.   ( )
An appreciation lesson.   ( )
Pilgrimages or trips.   ( )
Memory work or drill.   ( )
Definite Bible study.   ( )
A period for written work or creative expression.   ( )

8. If you are a departmental superintendent, consider thoughtfully each teacher in the department. Placing initials or numbers at the head of each column in the following chart to represent each of these teachers, check each in his proper column. If you are a teacher, check only in the first column for yourself.

Do I (or they) possess these qualities as a teacher?

                                  ( ) ( ) ( ) ( )

Christian motivation.
Considerateness.
Attractiveness.
Co-operation.
Enthusiasm.
Forcefulness.
Good judgment.
Industry.
Neatness.
Promptness.
Dependability.
Breadth of interest.
Patience.
Resourcefulness.
Objectivity.
Sympathetic understanding.
Honesty.
A sense of humor.
Adaptability.
Loyalty to the church.

9. If you are a teacher, check for yourself each of the following which you do in connection with your class group; if you are a departmental superintendent, check those which each teacher in your department does as a part of his teaching task.

The function of a teacher is:

	( )	( )	( )	( )
To keep pupils' growth the major aim.				
To make each pupil feel at home in the class group.				
To join with and encourage class activities.				
To keep on lookout for interesting projects.				
To steer group tactfully but not to dominate situation.				
To be on the lookout for interesting source materials.				
To guide the group in finding answers to puzzling problems.				
To give skillful personal counsel when pupils need guidance.				
To influence pupils by his own Christian living.				
To know how to guide active impulses of group into constructive channels.				
To co-operate with other leaders in department and church.				
To build up loyalty to department and church, not to center it around himself.				
To understand how to deal constructively with problem pupils.				

10. Which of the following means for leadership education have you used for yourself (if you are a teacher) or have been used in your department (if you are a superintendent)?

Leadership education class in church or community. ( )
Departmental conferences. ( )
Personal interviews. ( )
Observation of other teachers at work. ( )
Rating yourself with a score card or rating scale. ( )
Personal conferences with other professional leaders. ( )
Reading of books, pamphlets, magazine articles, and
    listening to radio talks, which deal with problems
    you meet as a leader. ( )
Attending conferences or conventions. ( )
Hearing inspirational talks which make you realize the
    importance of your work in the Church School. ( )
Attending a laboratory school. ( )
                               ( )

11. How is your department or class organized:

Does the department follow the correlated plan? ( )
Does it follow the unified plan? ( )
Does the department have representation on a Church
    School council? ( )
Does the class have a representative on the depart-
    mental council? ( )
Does the Intermediate Department have representa-
    tion in a young people's organization within the
    church? ( )
Does the department have definite standards for pro-
    motion to the Senior Department? ( )
What is the size of your class groups? ( )
Are the classes mixed, boys and girls? ( )
Is the class organized? ( )

12. What about the rooms and equipment provided:

Are your rooms and equipment satisfactory?   ( )
If not, are you making the very best possible use of
    what you have?   ( )

Do you have a separate departmental room?

Do you have separate classrooms?   ( )
Do you meet in the church auditorium?   ( )
Do you meet in combined session for worship with
    some other department or departments?   ( )

Which of the following do you have for use?

Chairs.	( )	Bulletin Board.	( )
Blackboards.	( )	Browsing Table or Li-	
Pictures.	( )	brary Nook.	( )
Worship Screen.	( )	Tables.	( )
Stage for Dramatics.	( )	Screens.	( )
Pencils and Notebooks.	( )	Cabinet for Supplies.	( )
Pews.	( )	Workshop.	( )
Maps.	( )	Other Materials.	( )

Place (*) after those items of equipment which you have
improvised or supplied for yourself. Place (**) after those
which you have asked for and had supplied by the Church
School board or department.

Which of the following types of records are kept in your department?

Attendance records.   ( )
Cumulative pupil records.   ( )
Logbook or diary, giving the record of teaching and
    learning experiences within the group.   ( )
Records of any check lists or tests given.   ( )
Records of teachers or prospective leaders for the de-
    partment.   ( )
Monthly or quarterly report for parents.   ( )
Quarterly or annual statistical report.   ( )
_____   ( )

13. What attempts to co-operate with other community organizations has your church or department made:

Have you sought to find out the objectives of these
  organizations?   ( )
Have you united with them in some community enterprise on which you could agree?   ( )
Have you planned your Pioneer program with these
  other programs involving your own group in mind?   ( )

Suggestions for Further Reading and Study

"Character and Religious Education Tests in Children's Work." Supplement to Research Bulletin No. 10.

Research Bulletin No. 10, "Measurement in the Church School." International Council of Religious Education, 1932.

INSTRUMENT FOR EXPLORING EXPERI-
ENCES OF BOYS AND GIRLS

Now let's get acquainted with:

1. *You and your family.*

a. Check in the list below the members of your family who live with you in your home:

Mother _____ Father _____ Sister _____ Brother _____
Grandmother _____ Grandfather _____ Others _____

b. What do you regularly do to help your family? _____

_____

c. Do you help by earning money? _____ How? _____

_____

d. What are some of the interesting things that you and your family do together? Check below:

Have picnics? _____ Take trips? _____ Read good books?
_____ Play games? _____ Visit friends? _____ Sing? _____
Enjoy music? _____ Worship? _____ Make plans for the home
together? _____ Study nature together? _____ Make gardens?
_____ Do things for others? _____ Listen to radio? _____ See
movies together? _____ Other things? _____

_____

2. *You and your free time.*

a. What games do you like to play? _____
Where do you play? Park? _____ Playground? _____ Back
yard? _____ Play streets? _____ Other streets? _____ Vacant
lots? _____ Alleys? _____ Other places? _____

b. Do you like to read? _____ What are your favorite books?

_____

Where do you get your books? Library? _____ Five and Ten
Cent Stores? _____ Own them? _____ Other sources? _____

_____

What magazines do you read? _____

Name your favorites. _____

   c. Do you read the newspaper? _____ What are your favorite parts? _____

   d. What are your favorite radio programs? _____

   e. Do you attend movies? _____ Once a week? _____ Several times a week? _____ Occasionally? _____ Where do you go to see movies? _____ Who are your favorite movie stars? _____

What recent pictures have you liked best? _____

   f. What do you like to do on Saturdays and holidays? _____

   g. What are your hobbies? Hiking? _____ Swimming? _____ Nature study? _____ Making things? _____ Being in plays? _____ Collecting things? _____ Drawing? _____ Music? _____ Writing stories or poetry? _____ Other things?

   h. Do you take any special lessons? Music? _____ Art? _____ Expression? _____ Dancing? _____

   i. What instrument do you play? _____

3. *You and your school.*

   a. What activities do you like best in school? _____

   b. What do you dislike the most? _____

   c. To what clubs do you belong at school? _____

   d. What school responsibilities do you hold? _____

4. *You and your church.*

   a. What church do you attend? _____ Regularly? _____ What Sunday School? _____ Regularly? _____

   b. Do your family attend church together? _____

   c. What do you like best about your Sunday School? _____

What do you dislike? _____

d. Have you ever attended Vacation Church School? _____
What do you like most about it? _____

e. To what church clubs do you belong?_____

5. *You and your community.*

a. What do you do to help to improve your community?

_____

b. What city affairs do you like to attend? Parades? _____
Band concerts? _____ Other affairs? _____

c. To what clubs do you belong? Scouts? _____ Camp Fire
Girls? _____ Y. W. or Y. M. C. A.? _____ Junior Red Cross?
_____ 4-H Club? _____ Other clubs (such as radio clubs, clubs
of your own group)? _____

d. Name several leading citizens of your community. _____

_____

e. What are your favorite world heroes? _____

_____

f. Would you like to tell us the names of some of your best
friends? _____

_____

Are there some things you would like to do, for which you
have no opportunity? _____ Name them. _____

_____

EXPLORING EXPERIENCES OF BOYS AND GIRLS [1]

1. *Public school experiences.*

a. Basic curriculum units in the social sciences, general science and nature study, music, art, and literature for this grade level.

(1) What goals or objectives are set forth in the printed syllabus? What evidence that they are in the thinking of the teachers of the local school? How do they fit in with the objectives of Christian education? How may they be supplemented?

(2) What textbooks or source books are recommended for use? Which are actually in use in the classrooms? What poems, stories, songs, pictures, are listed for use in this grade?

(3) What activities or projects are suggested in the syllabus? Which are actually carried out in the classrooms?

(4) What is the attitude of members of the group toward the projects? toward the entire situation in the schoolroom?

b. Celebration of special days in school, e.g., Armistice Day.

(1) What point of view is emphasized?

(2) What opportunity for a religious interpretation of these experiences is afforded the religious teacher?

c. School organization.

(1) Is it formal and teacher-centered, with a minimum of pupil purposing and participation?

(2) Is it democratic and informal, with opportunities for pupils' initiation of enterprises?

[1] "Selecting and Using Curriculum Materials in the Weekday Church School." Service Bulletin No. 620. International Council of Religious Education, 1937. Used by permission.

d. Music, art, and literature.

(1) Is material with religious value being taught in the school?

(2) Is this material used to interpret the other studies?

2. *Church and Church School experiences.*

a. General data.

(1) What different churches and Church Schools are represented in the group?

(2) How many of the boys and girls have no church connections?

(3) Which have only casual or infrequent connections with church life?

(4) What are the reasons for lack of church relations?

b. Points of view represented in these churches.

(1) Strong conservative or fundamentalist tendencies?

(2) Liberal or fairly tolerant attitudes?

(3) What special doctrinal points are held by these churches?

c. Sunday School courses used in the departments represented.

(1) International Uniform lessons?

(2) Catechetical instruction?

(3) Closely Graded, Group, or Departmental Graded denominational materials?

(4) Nondenominational materials?

d. Actual lessons being used at this time in the Sunday School classes represented in Weekday Church School classes.

(1) Are they life-centered?

(2) Are they predominantly Biblical?

(3) What methods are employed?

e. Other organizations in the church to which the pupils belong.

(1) Missionary society?

(2) Junior Christian Endeavor?

(3) Confirmation classes?

f. Church attendance of boys and girls.

(1) How many attend church?

(2) Do they think the service helpful to them?

(3) What kind of religious ideas are they gaining from their church experience?

(4) Do they harmonize or conflict with ideas gained in the public school?

3. *Home and family experiences.*

a. General data.

(1) What is the nationality of the pupils?

(2) Economic status of the homes?

(3) Cultural level?

(4) Religious practices?

(5) Is the home divided on questions of religion?

(6) Are there reading materials, play materials, a radio, music, in the home? If so, of what nature and quality?

(7) What is the social life between various members of the family?

b. Relation of parents to public school, church, Weekday Church School.

(1) Is it sympathetic and intelligent?

(2) Antagonistic?

(3) Indifferent?

(4) Are contacts easily established with parents?

(5) Is there any organization through which these may be accomplished?

(6) Is it done through calls in the home?

4. *Community and wider experience* (outside church, school, and home).

a. Movies in the neighborhood.

(1) Is educational supervision exercised over them?

(2) How frequently do children attend?

(3) What pictures have made the strongest impression on them?

(4) What are some of the best movies which might be referred to as source materials?

(5) What need is felt for evaluating the pictures seen?

(6) What pictures have children in the group seen recently?

b. Other recreational centers in the community.

(1) What centers are available to children in groups?

(2) Do the children attend?

(3) Are these centers well supervised?

(4) What social and religious activities are carried on?

c. Clubs or community organizations.

(1) To what organizations of this type do the children belong?

(2) What are the aims and objectives of these clubs?

(3) Are their purposes harmonious or conflicting with the purposes of school, church, home, and Weekday Church School?

d. Other community resources available to boys and girls.

(1) Is there an adequate library?

(2) An art museum?

(3) A child health center?

(4) A child guidance clinic?

(5) How many children of the group use these available resources?

e. What opportunities for travel, interesting vacation experiences, et cetera, have the children had?